Strategy and Corporate Governance

Strategy and Corporate Governance

The Formulation of Corporate and Business-Unit Strategies

Warnock Davies

BEP

BUSINESS EXPERT PRESS

Leader in applied, concise business books

Strategy and Corporate Governance:
The Formulation of Corporate and Business-Unit Strategies

Cover design by Clive G. Chen and Warnock Davies

Interior design by S4Carlisle Publishing Services, Chennai, India

First published in 2025 by
Business Expert Press, LLC
222 East 46th Street, New York, NY 10017
www.businessexpertpress.com

ISBN-13: 978-1-63742-904-4 (paperback)
ISBN-13: 978-1-63742-905-1 (e-book)

Strategic Management Collection

First edition: 2025

10 9 8 7 6 5 4 3 2 1

EU SAFETY REPRESENTATIVE
Mare Nostrum Group B.V.
Mauritskade 21D
1091 GC Amsterdam
The Netherlands
gpsr@mare-nostrum.co.uk

Description

Strategy and Corporate Governance provides managers, executives, board members, and consultants with concise and incisive information on:

- What strategy is and how it works;
- Corporate and business-unit strategies, their formulation, and their functionality in the conduct of corporate governance;
- The dichotomous pairs (DPs) method—and its use in the formulation of corporate and business-unit strategies, strategy-related decision-making, strategy analysis, and the modification of existing strategies;
- Core DPs that are used in the formulation of a wide range of corporate and business-unit strategies; and
- Ancillary factors that affect strategy formulation, implementation, and sustainability.

The book was written and formatted for use as a handbook and reference book—and for use as a text in executive development programs, MBA programs, and in-company seminars.

Contents

List of Figures

Acknowledgments

The author would like to thank his colleague and coauthor on a previous book, Clive Chen, for his extensive and invaluable assistance with the preparation of this book.

The author would also like to thank Business Expert Press, and especially Scott Isenberg, managing executive editor; John Pearce, editor of the Strategic Management collection; Charlene Kronstedt, production director; and Gajalakshmi Sivakumar and her team at S4Carlisle Publishing Services—for their important contributions during the publication of the book.

PART 1

Introduction

CHAPTER 1

Strategy and Corporate Governance

Contents

1.1   Corporate and Business-Unit Strategies

The term *strategy* can be defined as a multielement plan for achieving one or more of an entity's policy goals or operational goals,[1] by maximizing the use of resources and tactics—and by configuring the plan's elements in mutually supportive and/or synergistic combinations.[2]

When referring to business strategies, the *entity* in this definition can be a corporation or a business unit within a corporation. The distinctions between corporate entities and business-unit entities, and between policy goals and operational goals, results in many types of business strategies—but, in practice, all business strategies can be conflated into two primary categories: (1) *corporate strategies*, which are multielement plans for achieving an entity's policy goals, and (2) *business-unit strategies*, which are multielement plans for achieving an entity's operational goals.

---

[1] Policy goals and operational goals are discussed in Chapter 2, Section 2.2.
[2] This definition, and the origins and use of the term, are discussed in Chapter 2, Section 2.3.

1.2   Corporate Governance

Merriam-Webster defines *governance* as "the act or process of governing or overseeing the control and direction of something (such as a country or an organization)."[3] When applied to the governance of a country, the term can refer to the sum total of the decisions and actions by the legislative and executive branches of a government.

When applied to a corporation, the term refers to the sum total of (1) the legislative decisions and actions by a corporation's board of directors and (2) the executive decisions and actions by the senior-level management of a corporation, or a business unit of a corporation, for the purpose of giving effect to the decisions that have been taken by the corporation's board or by the senior-level management of the business unit.

Two of the primary functions of corporate governance are the development of policies that define an entity's purpose or reason for existing, its raison d'être, and that define the industry and geographical area of domain (AOD) where the entity will operate. For example, BYD Auto is the world's largest manufacturer of electric vehicles (EVs); its industry AOD is the manufacture and marketing of EV cars, buses, and trucks; its geographical AOD is 70 countries on six continents (which include the United States for buses and trucks but not for cars).

In levels of importance, these corporate governance functions are followed closely by the development of an entity's policy goals and operational goals. As discussed in Chapter 2, Section 2.2, the responsibility for establishing policy goals rests with a company's board of directors. The responsibility for establishing operational goals rests with a company's board, with its senior-level management, or with the senior-level management of a business unit.

1.3   Corporate Governance and Strategy Formulation

Corporate governance also includes the formulation and implementation of corporate strategies and business-unit strategies for achieving an entity's policy goals and operational goals. As discussed in Chapter 2,

---

[3] Merriam-Webster.com Dictionary, s.v. "governance."

Section 2.3, the responsibility for the performance of strategy formulation functions rests primarily with an entity's senior-level executives—who are the corporate equivalents of the *strategoi* in the ancient Greek city-states.

The strategy formulation process can, however, require and include participation by managers and executives at multiple levels, and by board members and/or consultants; and, to be effective, requires that

- all participants in the process, at all levels, share the same understanding of what strategy is and how it works;
- all participants in the process are on the same page when it comes to terms, principles, practices, and divisions of responsibility;
- all participants are familiar with corporate governance factors that can affect and/or be affected by corporate and business-unit strategies; and that
- executives and members of strategy teams are familiar with an advanced method for the formulation of corporate and business-unit strategies.

1.4   About This Book

This book was written for use as a handbook and reference book by managers, executives, board members, and consultants—and for use as a text in executive programs, MBA programs, and in-company seminars. The book addresses all of the criteria covered in the previous paragraph, by providing concise and incisive information on:

- What strategy is and how it works—and related terms, principles, and practices;
- Corporate and business-unit strategies, their functionality in the conduct of corporate governance, and related divisions of responsibility;
- Strategy formulation, the dichotomous pairs (DPs) method, and the use of the method in the formulation of corporate and business-unit strategies, strategy-related decision-making, strategy analysis, and the modification of existing strategies;

- Core DPs that are used in the formulation of a wide range of corporate and business-unit strategies; and
- Ancillary factors that affect strategy formulation, implementation, and sustainability.

The book includes four parts:

Part 1: Introduction. The chapters in this part discuss corporate and business-unit strategies and their functionality in the conduct of corporate governance; and the forms, functions, and causalities of strategy and the other elements in the GSRT framework.

Part 2: Strategy formulation. The chapters in this part discuss the DPs method and its use in the formulation of corporate and business-unit strategies—which includes the selection, weighting, and configuration of elements; the goal identification, clarification, and confirmation that precedes strategy formulation; and the feasibility and sustainability checking that precedes strategy implementation—and the use of the DPs method in strategy-related decision-making, strategy analysis, and the modification of existing strategies.

Part 3: Core DPs. This part includes three chapters, which discuss general core DPs, manufacturing core DPs, and marketing core DPs that can be used in the formulation of a wide range of corporate and business-unit strategies.

Part 4: Ancillary factors. This part includes chapters on life-cycle positions and elements from the game theory dichotomy, which can affect the formulation, implementation, and sustainability of corporate and business-unit strategies.

Examples:
The material covered in the book has been informed by the author's work in strategy formulation and corporate governance. The author did not, however, participate in any of the examples cited in the book.

CHAPTER 2

The GSRT Framework

Contents

Strategy can be defined as a multielement plan for achieving one or more of an entity's goals, by maximizing the use of resources and tactics—and by configuring the plan's elements in mutually supportive and/or synergistic combinations.

2.1   The Framework

In the social sciences, the term *dependent variable* refers to the thing that is to be achieved; the term *independent variable* refers to a factor that supports or facilitates, or works against, achieving the dependent variable. In the above definition, the dependent variable is an entity's goals; the independent variables are strategy, resources, and tactics.

These four variables—goals, strategy, resources, and tactics (GSRT)—can be seen as forming a conceptual framework that can help explain what strategy is and how it works, and can be used to facilitate the formulation of all types of strategies, including all types of business strategies. The elements of the GSRT framework correspond to the four *causal types* that Aristotle discussed in Metaphysics 1013a: *final cause*, goals (τέλος or télos); *formal cause*, strategy (μορφή or eîdos); *material cause*, resources (ὕλη or hûlē); and *efficient cause*, tactics (κίνησις or kinoûn).

The GSRT framework can be rendered graphically, using arrows of causality that run from cause to effect. In Figure 2.1, the arrows indicate the causal and functional relationships between each element and the other elements.

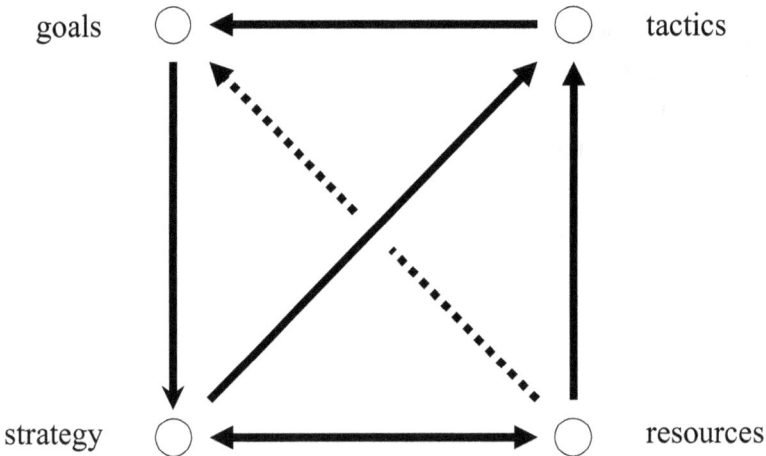

Figure 2.1. The GSRT framework

During the formulation of business strategies, the GSRT framework can be used (1) to identify and differentiate goals, strategy, resources, and tactics; (2) to facilitate communication and collaboration among participants in the process (which can include managers, executives, board members, and/or consultants); (3) to facilitate the selection and relative weighting of a strategy's elements; (4) to facilitate the configuration of a strategy's elements into mutually supportive and/or synergistic combinations; and (5) to review strategies for implementation feasibility, effectiveness, sustainability and/or approval.

2.2   Goals

Because business strategies are multielement plans for achieving one or more of an entity's policy goals or operational goals; and because in Aristotle's causal types goals are the *final cause* (or *telos*) that define the end objective that is to be achieved—goals are the dependent variable that drives (or should drive) every aspect of the formulation and implementation of every business strategy.

And because the discussion of any process must begin by establishing and clarifying the dependent variable, the discussion of strategy and corporate governance must begin by focusing on the nature and functionalities of policy goals and operational goals.

For these reasons, and because the causal relationships between goals and the other elements of the GSRT framework are central to the formulation of business strategies, the goals element is in the first position in the GSRT framework.

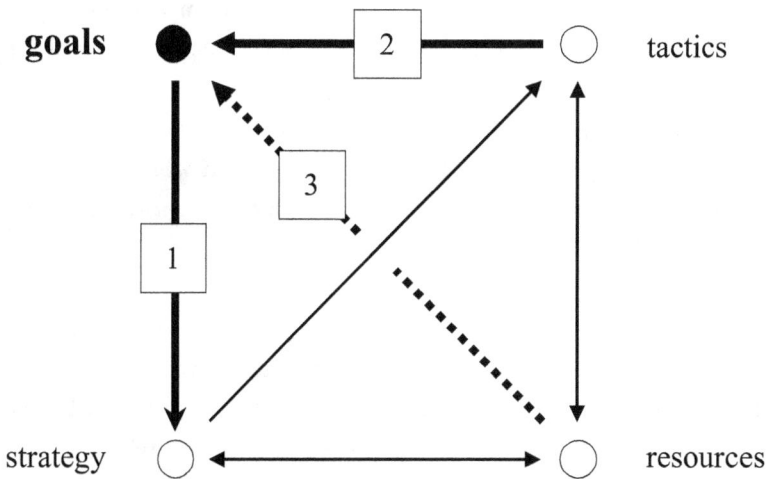

Figure 2.2. Goals in the GSRT framework

In Figure 2.2, arrow number [1] indicates that, in business entities, policy goals and operational goals drive the formulation of strategies. It follows, therefore, that it is difficult to formulate a strategy when the antecedent goal is ambiguous and/or poorly defined; and it is impossible to formulate a strategy when an antecedent goal has not been defined.

Arrow number [2] indicates that companies and their business units use tactics to achieve policy goals and operational goals by implementing strategies, and by delivering and operationalizing the use of resources.

Arrow number [3] indicates that some resources (such as company and product reputations) can in some situations be partially or fully self-operationalizing, and can have a direct causal relationship with policy goals and/or operational goals. As discussed in Section 2.4, arrow number [3] is dotted because in most situations resources are not self-operationalizing, but require the use of tactics to be delivered and operationalized. The delivery and operationalization dependency of resources on tactics is indicated by arrow numbers [2] and [3] in Figure 2.5.

Because the goals element is the dependent variable in strategy formulation and in the GSRT framework, the first step when formulating business strategies (or formulating any strategy) must always be to identify, clarify, and confirm the antecedent policy goal or operational goal that the strategy is intended to achieve. As discussed in Chapter 4, Section 4.1, one of the most common flaws in the formulation of business strategies is due to attempts by executives or strategy teams to formulate and implement a strategy when the antecedent policy goal or operational goal has not been identified, clarified, and confirmed.

The primacy of the goals element in the GSRT framework is similar to the emphasis on goals by Peter Drucker, in his work on *management by objectives*, and by Igor Ansoff in his formative work on *strategic management*.

2.2.1   Policy Goals

The term *policy goals* refers to goals that are adopted by a company's board. The term indicates that these goals are adopted by the entity's legislative body, as distinct from goals that are developed by the entity's executives. The term *policy* and its usage are from the ancient Greek city-states, and especially the Athens city-state, where the legislative assembly, the *polis*, was responsible for adopting, inter alia, resolutions that created social, civic, and military goals. A company's policy goals can originate from within its board of directors, or can be proposed to the board by corporate or business-unit senior-level management.

In many cases, policy goals are not presented as goals per se, but are presented as policies or policy decisions. For example, in 2023, General Motors announced it would discontinue the manufacture of cars in Australia, which made public an AOD policy decision that had been adopted by the company's board. Because this new GM AOD policy had not been put into effect at the time it was announced, it was an AOD policy goal.

2.2.2 Related and Quasi-Related Terms

Two corporate governance terms, which have a direct relationship with policy and policy goals, are *vision* and *mission*. Three other terms, which are seemingly related to policies and policy goals, but are in fact related to operational goals and/or operations management,[4] are *policy positions*, *operating* or *managerial policies*, and *policy slogans*.

a. Vision

Vision is seeing a desired future situation. When talking about art, religion, science, social structures, and politics, Jean-Paul Sartre defined vision as the ability to think of what is not. In corporate governance, vision can provide the conceptual precursor for creating an entity's purpose or reason for existing, its area of domain, or other corporate or business-unit policies—by providing an image of what a company or business-unit will be, what it will do, and where it will do it.

b. Mission

A company's mission defines the entity's purpose or reason for existing, its raison d'être. In corporate governance, a mission statement can provide board members and senior-level management with a benchmark for policy decision-making, and provides a means for communicating a company's raison d'être to its internal and external constituents. Mission statements frequently focus on an entity's primary policy goals and its AOD.

---

[4] The terms *operations* and *operational goals* are discussed in Section 2.3.

c. Policy positions

A policy position is an official statement of an entity's values, beliefs, and/or commitments. Policy positions can refer to an entity's hiring practices, professional ethics, customer service, or the environment—and can also define an entity's position on, or response to, a specific issue. References to policy positions can result in what appears to be policy-strategy inversion, where the word *policy* is applied to the means for achieving the goal. In most cases that appear to be policy-strategy inversion, the term policy refers to a *policy position* or to an *operating policy* or *managerial policy*.

d. Operating or managerial policies

An operating or managerial policy is a rule, regulation, guideline, and/or standard that governs some aspect of an entity's operations, which can be internal or external. For example, a company's *employee travel policy*, and a retailer's *return and exchange policy*, are operating or managerial policies. In a small percentage of cases, operating or managerial policies (and policy positions) have been adopted by a company's board, and are, therefore, literally policies—but in the vast majority of cases they have been created by the senior-level management of a business unit, and are either methods resources or tactics.[5]

e. Policy slogans

A policy slogan is frequently repeated phrase, which is used to present and/or promote a particular characteristic of a company, its operations, and/or its products; to present and/or promote a company's values and/or standards; to motivate employees, suppliers, and/or strategic alliance (SA) partners; and/or to strengthen a company's relations with one or more of its host communities. Policy slogans can be important and effective communication, marketing, leadership, and motivational tools. In some cases, a policy slogan may look like a corporate or business-unit policy; they are, however (like most policy positions and operating or managerial policies) either methods resources or tactics.

---

[5] Methods resources are discussed in Section 2.4.2; tactics are discussed in Section 2.5.

2.2.3 Operational Goals

The term *operations* in most cases refers to a company's revenue-generating activities, which in larger companies occur within the entity's business units. Operations can include the design, development, manufacture, and/or marketing of industrial and consumer products (and parts and components for industrial and consumer products); growing, harvesting, processing, and marketing agricultural products; oil, coal, and metals exploration, extraction (drilling and mining), processing, and marketing; and the design, development, and delivery of services. Any goal that is related to any of these functions can be seen as an operational goal. Some financial management, human resources management, and physical resources management functions that are associated with operational functions are also seen as being operations, even though they may not, in and of themselves, be a revenue-generating activity.

Some operational goals are created by a company's board of directors—but in most cases they are created by a company's senior-level management, or by the senior-level management of a business unit. Because some policy goals address directly an entity's operations (such as GM's AOD policy goal for the discontinuation of car manufacturing in Australia), they can look like, and are often treated as, operational goals.

As discussed in Section 2.2.1, the adoption of policy goals by a company's board of directors is a legislative function, which mirrors the adoption of social, civic, and military goals by the legislative body (*polis*) in the ancient Greek city-states. If an operational goal is adopted or formally approved by a company's board, it can also be seen as a legislative function; but if the operational goal is created or approved by an entity's senior-level management, it is an executive function.

2.3   Strategy

The term *strategy* can be defined as a multielement plan for achieving one or more of an entity's policy or operational goals by maximizing the use of resources and tactics and by configuring the plan's elements in mutually supportive and/or synergistic combinations. The term and its usage (like the term policy) are from the ancient Greek city-states (and especially the Athens city-state), where it referred to a multielement plan that was formulated and implemented by generals (*strategoi*) for the purpose of achieving a military policy goal that had been adopted by the legislative body (*polis*). In Aristotle's causal types, strategy is the *formal cause*, which provides the form, pattern, or plan that arranges the use of the *material cause* (resources) and *efficient cause* (tactics) that result in achieving the *final cause* (goals).

The formulation and implementation of business strategies (like the multielement plans formulated by the *strategoi* in the Greek city-states) is an executive function; the responsibility for performing this function rests with a company's senior-level management.

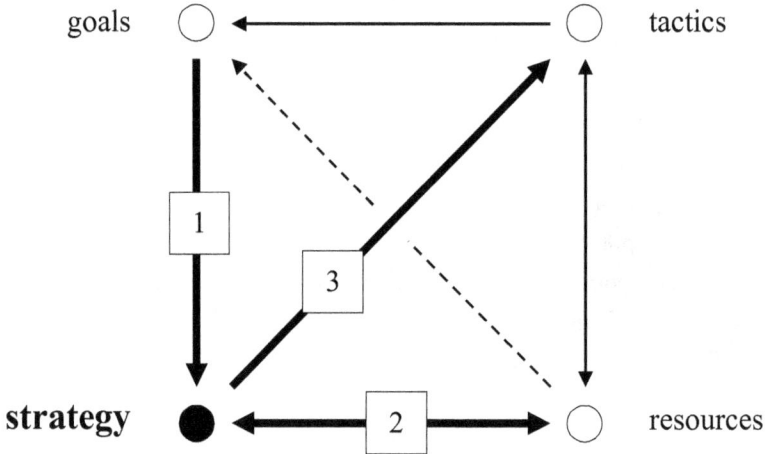

Figure 2.3. Strategy in the GSRT framework

In Figure 2.3, arrow number [1] indicates that (1) a business entity's policy goals drive the formulation of its corporate strategies and (2) an entity's operational goals drive the formulation of its business-unit strategies.

Arrow number [2] is double-headed, which indicates there is a two-way causal relationship between strategies and resources. The arrow of causality that runs from resources to strategy [←] indicates that resources are a sine qua non of strategy, and that strategy formulation is dependent on the availability of resources. The arrow of causality that runs from strategy to resources [→] indicates that (1) strategies drive decisions related to the acquisition and development of resources; (2) strategies drive the choice and use of resources; and (3) a function of strategies is the maximization of the use of resources.

Arrow number [3] indicates that (1) strategies drive the choice and use of tactics and (2) companies and their business units use tactics to implement strategies.

2.3.1   Corporate and Business-Unit Strategies

As discussed in Chapter 1, the entity referred to in the above strategy definition can be a corporation, or a business unit within a corporation— which results in two primary groups of business strategies: (1) *corporate strategies*, which are strategies for achieving policy goals, and (2) *business-unit strategies*, which are strategies for achieving operational goals.

Corporate strategies are multielement plans for achieving policy goals. As discussed in Section 2.2, policy is a legislative function, and goals that have been adopted by a company's board of directors are referred to as policy goals. When the purpose of a strategy is to achieve one or more of a company's policy goals, it is referred to as a corporate strategy. It is important to note that they are not called corporate strategies because they apply to the entire company. In fact, many corporate strategies do not apply to an entire company, but apply to a single division, subsidiary, business unit, group of business units, or to a product group or a single product. The reason they are called *corporate strategies* is because their purpose is to achieve one or more of a corporation's policy goals.

Business-unit strategies are multielement plans that are designed to achieve one or more operational goals of a division, subsidiary, or other business unit; or to achieve a product- or service-related operational goal. Some operational goals that drive business-unit strategies are created by a company's board of directors, but in most cases they are created by a company's senior-level management, or by the senior-level management of a business unit. Business-unit strategies can include marketing strategies, manufacturing strategies, human resources strategies, and financial management strategies—and subsets of these strategies, which can include product pricing strategies, supply chain management strategies, human resources retention strategies, and taxation abatement strategies.

2.3.1.1   Distinctions and Similarities

The primary difference between corporate strategies and business-unit strategies is that (1) in corporate strategies, the dependent variable is to achieve one or more of an entity's policy goals and (2) in business-unit strategies, the dependent variable is to achieve one or more of an entity's operational goals.

This primary difference notwithstanding, corporate strategies and business-unit strategies share important similarities. Both are multielement plans—and the independent variables, in both types, include (1) the maximization of the use of resources and tactics and (2) the configuration of the plan's elements in mutually supportive and/or synergistic combinations.

When a business-unit strategy addresses the same area as a corporate strategy, the business-unit strategy may be an element in the corporate strategy. At small and midsize companies that are operated as a single business unit, it can sometimes be difficult to distinguish between corporate strategy and business-unit strategy, but the criteria provided in Section 2.3.1 and in this section also apply to these companies.

2.3.1.2   Response Strategies

When the purpose of a business strategy is to address and correct an unsatisfactory operational situation or problem, it can be referred to as a *response strategy* or *problem-solving strategy*, or colloquially as a *troubleshooting strategy*. When the purpose of a response strategy is to reverse the operational decline of a company or business unit, it is referred to as a *turnaround strategy*. Response strategies are not a third category, but are a subcategory of either corporate strategies or business-unit strategies. In the case of turnaround strategies, they can include a mix of both corporate strategies and business-unit strategies. Because most situations that require the formulation and implementation of a response strategy are operational, most response strategies are business-unit strategies. In some response strategies, and often with turnaround strategies, the situation requires the adoption of a policy goal by a company's board of directors, which can require the formulation and implementation of a corporate response strategy.

2.3.2   The Primary Characteristics

Strategies can be seen as having several characteristics that reflect the original meaning of the term, and that distinguish them from other plans. Two of these characteristics are stated in the above definition, another is implied in the above definition, and some characteristics apply only to some strategies.

a. Multielement plans

A fundamental characteristic of all strategies, which dates from the strategies formulated and implemented by the *strategoi* in the ancient Greek city-states, is that they include multiple elements. If a plan does not include multiple elements, ipso facto, it is not a strategy.

For many managers, executives, board members, and consultants, the multielement characteristic can be problematic, because (1) the multielement complexity of strategies is antithetical to the *keep it simple* mantra and (2) there is a widespread preference among managers and executives, and even some board members, for single-element "silver-bullet" solutions. This complexity aversion is not new. In his 1964 article, "The Concept of the Marketing Mix," where he coined the term, Neil Borden says the reason he wrote the article was to counter the tendency among marketing managers and executives to focus solely on advertising, and to ignore the other 11 elements that should be included when formulating marketing strategies. And complexity aversion is why the 12 elements contained in Borden's original "Marketing Mix" have been reduced to the 4P's of marketing.

b. Mutually supportive and/or synergistic combinations

A second characteristic that distinguished the multielement plans that were formulated by the *strategoi* is that the plan's elements were chosen and configured so they would be at least mutually supportive and preferably would be synergistic. These combinations are discussed in Chapter 3. Sections 3.6.1 and 3.6.2.

c. Situation specific

Because the purpose of a business strategy is to achieve one or more specific goals, at a specific entity, in a specific industry, and under a specific set of conditions—or to respond to a particular situation[6]—we can say that all business strategies are situation specific.

d. Time sensitive

Because strategies are formulated and implemented for the purpose of achieving one or more specific goals that occur at a specific time; because response strategies are formulated to address a situation or problem that has occurred at a particular time; and because product, industry, and company life-cycles positions change over time;[7] we can say that strategies are time sensitive. Because strategies are time sensitive, a strategy that was formulated and used to address a goal situation at a previous time may not be successful if used to address a current goal situation, even if the two goal situations are ostensibly similar or the same.

e. Nonlinearity and indirect or circuitous routes

One of the characteristics that has historically been associated with both military and nonmilitary strategies has been nonlinearity. Linear plans, which have the advantage of relative simplicity, follow a single relatively straight path, employ an ordered sequence of actions, and are driven by a single outcome. Some strategies, however, employ a nonlinear sequence, which can include parallel or alternative paths, can allow paths to include more than one option, and in some cases allow for more than one outcome. Also, the multielement plans that were developed by the *strategoi* in the Greek city-states sometimes included radical nonlinear elements, which could include taking an indirect or multistep circuitous route to achieve a goal or objective. More recently, in 1971, when China felt threatened militarily by the USSR, Chairman Mao Zedong responded strategically, invoked a traditional nonlinear Chinese proverb, "make friends with the enemy far away to defeat the enemy at the gate," and used a visit by the US Table Tennis team to initiate relations with the United States.

---

[6] Response strategies are discussed in Section 2.3.1.2.

[7] Product, company, and industry life-cycle positions are discussed in Chapter 9.

f. Secrecy

Sharing privileged information is one of the functional characteristics of strategic alliances,[8] and companies that are engaged in
SAs frequently share information concerning their business-unit
strategies. What works in plus-sum situations, however, does not
work in zero-sum competitive situations, and most business strategies are competitive zero-sum games.[9] For an executive to reveal
their company's competitive strategy, when they are engaged in a
competitive business environment, would be as foolish as a general making public their plan for defeating the enemy. Companies
frequently discuss their policy goals, and may even discuss their
resources—but because most companies operate in a competitive
zero-sum environment, well-managed companies rarely discuss
their strategies.

g. Complexity and difficulty

Some of the characteristics listed in this section, and especially the
mutually supportive and/or synergistic combinations characteristic,
and the nonlinear characteristic, can make strategies more complex
to design and more difficult to implement than single-element
linear plans. But these seemingly negative characteristics make
strategies more effective in complex environments, more flexible in
diverse situations, and more able to maximize the use of an entity's
resources and tactics. Because of this, strategies are able to achieve
policy goals and operational goals that cannot be achieved by using
single-element linear plans.

2.3.3 Strategy-Related Terms

The word *strategy* and its derivatives are widely used terms, the meanings
of which in many cases are not remotely related to the above definition

---

[8] Strategic alliances are discussed in Chapter 6, Section 6.4.2; and in Chapter 10,
Section 10.4.1.
[9] Zero-sum and plus-sum games are discussed in Chapter 10.

of strategy. There are, however, several strategy-related usages that deserve special mention.

a. Strategic intent

The term *strategic intent*, which was coined by Gary Hamel and C. K. Prahalad, refers to the objective that is to be achieved (Hamel and Prahalad 1989, 63–76), which Aristotle called the *final cause*, and which is synonymous with the *goals* element in the GSRT framework.

b. Strategy and long-term

In business strategic planning, the term *strategic* is used as an adjective to mean long term. But the terms *strategic* and *long term* are not synonymous. For example, when a company uses corporate divestiture and/or acquisition strategies to change its AOD, these actions and activities are strategic, but they can be effected over the short term; conversely, many long-term business activities are tactical, not strategic. Because a strategy can be defined as a plan for achieving policy or operational goals, planning that is long term may or may not be strategic—depending on if its purpose is or is not related to achieving one or more of an entity's policy or operational goals.

c. Strategic thinking

The term *strategic thinking* (or *thinking strategically*) can refer to one or more of the primary characteristics of strategy that are discussed in Section 2.3.2, including the multielement characteristic discussed in Section 2.3.2 (a), or the nonlinear and indirect or circuitous routes characteristic discussed in Section 2.3.2 (e). But because a strategy can be defined as a plan for achieving an entity's policy or operational goals, a more general and fundamental meaning of the term *strategic thinking* would be "goal-related thinking" or "goal-driven thinking," which distinguishes strategic thinking from tactical thinking.

d. Strategic management

The "goal-related thinking" or "goal-driven thinking," which distinguishes strategic thinking from tactical thinking, was a central factor in Peter Drucker's original work on *management by objectives*, and continued in the formative work by Igor Ansoff and others on *strategic management*. The term strategic management can, therefore, be defined as "goal-related management" or "goal-driven management."

e. Strategy and methods resources

The term strategy is sometimes applied to what are, in fact, methods resources, which are discussed in Section 2.4.2. For example, some proponents of Kaizen, Total Quality Management (TQM), Six Sigma, Just-In-Time supply chain methods (JIT), Quality Circles, benchmarking, best practices, outsourcing, lean manufacturing, and business reengineering have presented these methods resources as strategies.

2.4   Resources

A resource can be defined as a thing that can be used to satisfy a need or want, produce an effect, or contribute to producing an effect. The most significant characteristic of resources in the functioning of the GSRT framework is their utility: their ability to be used by strategies and tactics to achieve an entity's policy goals and/or operational goals. In Aristotle's causal types, resources are the *material cause*, which is used by the *formal cause* (strategy) and the *efficient cause* (tactics) to achieve the *final cause* (policy goals and operational goals).

In the GSRT framework, resources are a sine qua non of strategy; without resources, strategy can achieve nothing. Resources provide the "with what" for achieving an entity's goals; they are the things that are delivered and operationalized by tactics to achieve policy goals.

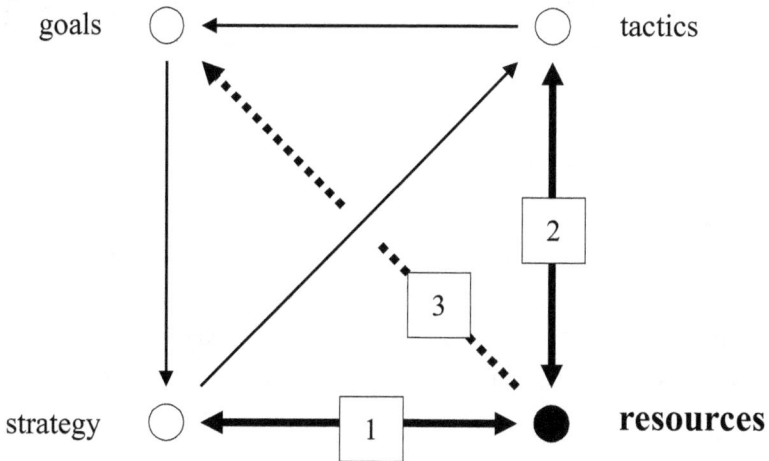

Figure 2.4. Resources in the GSRT framework

In Figure 2.4, arrow number [1] is double-headed, which indicates there is a two-way causal relationship between resources and strategies. The arrow of causality that runs from resources to strategy [←] indicates that resources are fundamental elements in the formulation of strategies. The arrow of causality that runs from strategy to resources [→] indicates that (1) strategies drive decisions related to the acquisition and development of resources, (2) strategies drive the choice and use of resources, and (3) resources are a critical factor in strategy implementation.

Arrow number [2] is also double-headed, which indicates there is a two-way causal relationship between resources and tactics. The arrow of causality that runs from resources to tactics [↑] indicates that tactics use resources to achieve policy goals and operational goals—by delivering and operationalizing resources. The arrow of causality that runs from tactics to resources [↓] indicates that tactics are used in the acquisition and development of resources.

Arrow number [3] indicates that, in some situations, some resources can have a direct causal relationship with policy goals and/or operational goals. In Figure 2.4, arrows [1] and [2] are solid, because they apply in all situations, but arrow number [3] is dotted, because in most situations resources require the use of tactics to be delivered and operationalized. This dependency of resources on tactics is indicated by arrows [2] and [3] in Figure 2.5. In some cases, a resource (such as a company or product reputation) can be partially or fully self-operationalizing. The dotted arrow number [3] in Figure 2.4 indicates that in these cases, the resource is able to self-deliver and to have a direct relationship with goals.

2.4.1 Types of Resources

Resources can be classified as tangible or intangible, and as internal (within the company) or external (outside the company). Resources can also be grouped into several categories or types, which include physical resources, financial resources, human resources, intellectual property resources, relationship resources, reputation resources, and methods resources.

a. Physical resources
   Physical resources include factories, warehouses, and office buildings; machine tools, manufacturing equipment, and production

lines; computers and office furniture and equipment; motor vehicles; and mines, forests, and farms.

b. Financial resources

Financial resources include cash on hand, income from the sale of products and/or services, revenue from other sources, retained earnings, the ownership of equity in other companies, the ownership of bonds and other financial instruments, the ability to borrow, and (in the case of publicly listed companies) the ability to generate equity capital through the sale of shares.

c. Human resources

Human resources include all of a company's full- and part-time employees, from entry-level employees to supervisors, managers, executives, board members, and consultants. A company's human resources can also be seen as including the employees of a company's distributors, suppliers, and/or SA partners.

d. Intellectual property resources

Intellectual property resources include patents, copyrights, and trademarks; product and process designs—which include, inter alia, a wide range of artificial intelligence (AI) products and programs; and manufacturing and marketing technologies.

e. Relationship resources

Relationship resources include relationships with each of a company's internal and external constituencies; alliances with other companies, supply chain management networks, and relationships with suppliers; outsourcing relationships, distribution networks, and relationships with distributors and retailers; and corporate social responsibility relationships, host community relationships, and employee relationships. Relationship resources can also include a company's relationships with the customers and end users of its products and/or services.

f. Reputation resources

Reputation resources include the reputation of a company and its products and/or services with each of its internal and external constituencies.

The different types of resource discussed in this section are not discrete; there can be overlap between two or more resource types and a high degree of interrelationship between resource types. For example, intellectual property resources and relationship resources involve the use of human resources and methods resources, the acquisition of most types of resources require the use of financial resources and/or relationship resources, and AI resources can cut across several or many resource types. As discussed in Chapters 7 and 8, operations-specific strategies use combinations of multiple types of resources.

2.4.2 Methods Resources

Methods resources can include methods related to corporate governance, corporate management, and business-unit management, and can be seen as placing on a continuum from more general to more specific. The following list begins with methods resources that are closer to the more general end of the continuum: manufacturing, marketing, financial management, and supply chain management methods; human resources management methods; outsourcing, motivational, negotiating, change management, and alliance management methods; benchmarking, best practices, business reengineering, core competency development, flexible/intelligent/agile manufacturing, and lean manufacturing methods; and Lean Production, Distributed-flexible Manufacturing, Process-Oriented Management, Total Cost Management, TQM, Six Sigma, JIT, Quality Circles, and Kaizen.

2.4.3 Core Competencies

A methods resource that is critical to the survival, success, and/or sustainability of a company or business-unit can be referred to as a core competency (CC). Core competencies include managerial, manufacturing, and marketing abilities and capabilities; and other areas of operational expertise that allow a company to achieve and maintain competitive advantage. The term *competitive advantage*, as used here, refers to a factor or combination of factors that provide a person, product, or company with an advantage when engaged in a competitive environment. The term does not indicate the degree of advantage provided; does not rank the advantage in relation to other advantages that the person, product, or company may have; and does not indicate the results of having this advantage. The term only says that, in a competitive situation, this factor could provide an advantage.

The term *core competencies* came into popular usage in the mid-1980s, and initially focused on a company's specialized expertise in research and development (R&D), product development, and/or manufacturing. Since then, the use of the term has been extended to include all areas of expertise that could affect the survival, success, and/or sustainability of a company or business unit.

2.4.3.1   CC Maximization and Acquisition

The function of core competencies in corporate and business-unit strategies can be seen as either CC maximization or CC acquisition. Core competency maximization focuses on using a company's core competencies in a way that will produce the greatest possible operating benefit. CC maximization can play a critical role in the formulation and implementation of competitive strategies, because it focuses on those areas of expertise that distinguish a company or business unit from its competitors—and are the basis for a company or business unit achieving and maintaining competitive advantage.

CC acquisition focuses on building or buying new core competencies to improve competitive advantage in the entity's current area of domain, or to facilitate the entity's migration into a new AOD. Because core competencies are methods resources, they influence the formulation of policies and strategies relating to what products the company or business unit will develop, manufacture, and/or market—and how those operations will be performed.

2.4.3.2   CCs and Area of Domain

A company or business unit can use CC maximization and/or acquisition within its present AOD to improve product quality, reduce costs, improve productivity, improve marketing and distribution, or in other ways improve the competitive position of the company or business unit. CC acquisition can also be used to change a company or business unit's industry AOD, and/or to change its geographical area of domain.

In the past, there was a widely held principle or belief that—because an entity's core competencies can be critical factors in its survival, success, and/or sustainability—an entity must maintain direct control of its CCs, and must, therefore, include its CCs in its industry AOD. Because of this principle or belief, companies and their business units rarely if ever outsourced their core competencies. But, as discussed in Chapter 7, Section 7.2.1, there are now many examples that indicate this principle or belief no-longer applies.

2.4.4   The Stand-Alone Use of Resources

As discussed in Section 2.4, resources are a sine qua non of strategy—without resources strategy can achieve nothing. In some cases, however, managers, executives, board members, and/or consultants place an inordinate emphasis on resources. This may be because having or not having the necessary quantity and/or quality of one or more of the resources from the list in Section 2.4.1 is frequently the determining variable in corporate and business-unit decision-making. Whatever the cause of this inordinate emphasis, its effect can lead some managers, executives, board members, and/or consultants—and especially those who want to avoid the time, complexity, and difficulty that can be associated with the formulation and implementation of business strategies—to attempt to achieve a policy or operational goal through the direct stand-alone application of resources. When this occurs, an entity's resources are not being used as an element of strategy but as a surrogate for strategy; and the use of the entity's resources are not being maximized.

An inordinate emphasis on resources can also result in goal–resources inversion during the strategy formulation process, when resources usurp the place of goals in the GSRT framework. As discussed in Section 2.4, the role of resources in the GSRT framework is to provide the things needed to implement strategies that achieve policy goals or operational goals. When this causality is inverted, the subject policy goal or operational goal is supplanted by the goal of maximizing the use of one or more resources. For example, the current ascendancy of AI, which is an intellectual property resource, can result in references to "AI-driven strategies," where the AI resource is presented as the policy or operational goal that drives strategy formulation (rather than as a resource that can be used by a strategy to achieve one or more policy or operational goals), and is, therefore, a case of goal–resources inversion.

2.5   Tactics

The term *tactics* refers to actions or activities that are intended to produce a specific effect or result. In the GSRT framework, tactics are the actions and/or activities business entities use to implement strategies, by delivering and operationalizing resources to achieve policy goals and/or operational goals. In Aristotle's causal types, tactics are the *efficient cause*, which is the agent, actions, or activities that are used by the *formal cause* (strategy), and that use the *material cause* (resources), to achieve the *final cause* (policy goals and operational goals).

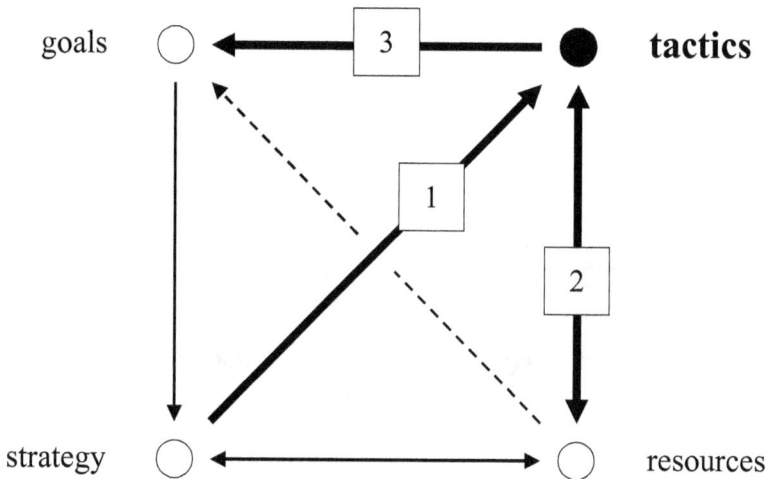

Figure 2.5. Tactics in the GSRT framework

In Figure 2.5, arrow number [1] indicates that (1) strategies drive the choice and use of tactics and (2) business entities use tactics to implement strategies.

Arrow number [2] is double-headed, which indicates there is a two-way causal relationship between tactics and resources. The arrow of causality that runs from resources to tactics [↑] indicates that resources are the things used by tactics to achieve policy goals and operational goals.

The arrow of causality that runs from tactics to resources [↓] indicates that tactics are used in the acquisition and development of resources.

Arrow number [3] indicates that business entities use tactics to achieve policy goals and operational goals: (1) by delivering and operationalizing the use of resources and (2) by implementing strategies.

Tactics, like resources, are a sine qua non of strategy; without tactics, strategy can achieve nothing. Tactics are the actions and/or activities that make it possible for companies to formulate and implement corporate strategies and business-unit strategies by delivering and operationalizing the use of resources. Resources and tactics are highly interdependent, because (in most cases) resources cannot be delivered and operationalized without the use of tactics, and tactics can achieve nothing without using resources.

2.5.1   Types of Tactics

Tactics can be classified as operational or facilitating, and, like resources, can also be classified as internal (within the company) or external (outside the company). Tactics can be grouped into more than a dozen main types. These include organizational behavior and management tactics; communication tactics; financial management tactics; human resources management tactics; alliance tactics; negotiation tactics; logistics tactics; product research, design, and development tactics; core competency and product acquisition tactics; company and business-unit acquisition tactics; manufacturing tactics; supply chain management tactics; outsourcing tactics; and marketing tactics.

As with resources, the different types of tactics discussed in this section are not discrete; there can be overlap between two or more types of tactics, and in many cases there is a high degree of interrelationship between types. Also each of these main types of tactics can include several or many subtypes of tactics. For example, marketing tactics can include consumer centered and competition driven tactics; product R&D tactics, pricing tactics, branding tactics, promotions tactics, and packaging tactics; channels of distribution tactics, personal selling tactics, advertising tactics, display tactics, servicing tactics, physical handling tactics, international marketing tactics, and market research tactics.

2.5.2   Strategy and Tactics

A frequent misuse of the term strategy occurs when the term strategy is applied to what are in fact tactics. This misuse of the term is not new: *The Art of War* by Sun Zi (the fifth century BCE classic from China), *The Prince* by Nicolo Machiavelli (the fourteenth century classic from Italy), and *The Book of Five Rings* by Miyamoto Musashi (the seventeenth century classic from Japan) are widely revered as seminal works on strategy. But each of these works is a compilation of recommendations relating to the use of tactics (or, in some cases, the use of resources and tactics), very few of which exhibit any of the other characteristics discussed in Section 2.3.2—and almost none are multielement plans, where the elements are configured in mutually supportive or synergistic combinations.

2.5.3   Resources and Tactics

The resources and tactics classifications are in some cases not discrete, because some "things that produce an effect, or contribute to producing an effect," which are classified as resources, can also be seen as tactics, because they are "actions or activities that are intended to produce an effect." Because of this definitional overlap, methods resources that have a high activity content are often referred to as tactics.

2.5.4   The Proclivity for Tactics

As discussed in Section 2.5, tactics are a sine qua non of strategy; without tactics, strategy can achieve nothing. But, as with resources, the critically important function of tactics in strategy formulation is in some cases offset by an inordinate operational emphasis on tactics.

The formulation of business strategies requires that executives and strategy teams focus on the antecedent policy goal or operational goal that the strategy is intended to achieve, on the selection of elements they will be included in a strategy, and on the configuration of those elements into mutually reinforcing and/or synergistic combinations.

In some cases, however, managers, executives, board members, and/or consultants are constrained by one or more factors that cause them to give inordinate emphasis to tactics, and to focus primarily on tactics rather than on the subject goal and the strategy for achieving that goal. These constraints can include a failure to understand the difference between strategy and tactics; the need at publicly listed companies to produce short-term results (which is also called *making the quarterly numbers*); and the tactical focus by the media and by some management gurus.

As with the stand-alone use of resources, giving an inordinate emphasis to tactics can lead some managers, executives, board members, and/or consultants to try to avoid the time, difficulty, and complexity that can be associated with the formulation and implementation of business strategies by attempting to use tactics to achieve a policy or operational goal. When this occurs, tactics are not being used as an element of strategy but as a surrogate for strategy.

PART 2

Strategy Formulation

CHAPTER 3

The DPs Method

Contents

Strategy can be defined as a multielement plan for achieving one or more of an entity's goals, by maximizing the use of resources and tactics—and by configuring the plan's elements in mutually supportive and/or synergistic combinations.

3.1   The Need for a Method

The central function in the formulation of all strategies, including all corporate strategies and business-unit strategies, is element selection. Other strategy formulation functions, which include the relative weighting of each of the selected elements (which is discussed in Section 3.5), the configuration of the selected elements into mutually supportive and/or synergistic combinations (which is discussed in Section 3.6), and the pre- and post-formulation functions that are discussed in Chapter 4, are all important parts of the strategy formulation process; and each of these other formulation-related functions can have very significant effects on the formulation, implementation, effectiveness, and sustainability of corporate and business-unit strategies. But none of these other functions can fix a business strategy if the element-selection process has not identified and included all of the necessary and appropriate elements.

In his 1948 seminal article, James Culliton refers to an executive who is engaged in strategy formulation as *a decider* and *a mixer of ingredients*. Culliton first calls the strategist a decider, because before an executive or strategy team can weight a strategy's multiple elements, and before they can configure the elements into mutually supportive and/or synergistic combinations, they must decide which elements to include in the mix.

Because element selection is the central function in strategy formulation; because the difference between a successful and unsuccessful strategy can be due to the absence or inclusion of a single element; because all strategies are situation specific and no two situations are the same (and elements that were used in a strategy that worked in an earlier ostensibly similar situation may not work in a strategy that is being formulated for a current situation); because the formulation and implementation of business strategies in many cases does not allow for second chances (or the second chance may come at a high price); and because the executives and team members who are engaged in the formulation of a strategy must, in many cases, be able to explain and defend how and why they chose to include (or not to include) a particular element in a strategy—those who are involved in the strategy formulation process must employ a rational, defendable, reliable, and effective method or algorithm when they are engaged in the selection of a strategy's constituent elements and other aspects of the strategy formulation process.

3.2   The Dichotomous Pairs Method

The dichotomous pairs (DPs) method includes four steps: (1) the identification of relevant DPs; (2) the selection of elements from each of the identified DPs; (3) the weighting of the selected elements; and (4) the configuration of the selected elements.[10]

In the DPs method, the term *dichotomous pair* refers to two distinct elements that are seen as possible functional alternatives, such as "specialized" and "diversified." In this book, DPs are referred to using compound nouns that contain a DP's two constituent elements linked by an ampersand, such as "specialized & diversified."[11] The two elements in a DP can be opposites from within a generic classification (as in the specialized & diversified DP), or can be alternatives from different generic classifications (as in the profits & growth DP). These DP divisions and other DP characteristics are discussed in Chapter 5, Section 5.1.

The DPs method allows an executive or strategy team to examine and evaluate a large number of elements for possible inclusion in a strategy—and to compare and select from a large number of possible combinations of elements. During the strategy formulation process, the DPs method (1) helps to ensure that all possible elements are considered and evaluated; (2) can be used to identify and clarify the significant characteristics of different elements, and facilitates the comparative evaluation of elements by accentuating the benefits and disadvantages of using each element; (3) helps to avoid element non-selection and wrong selection; (4) allows for the appropriate comparative weighting of a strategy's constituent elements; (5) facilitates the configuring of elements in mutually supportive and/or synergistic combinations; (6) facilitates communication, process participation, and reporting; (7) provides flexibility and options by

---

[10] In addition to these four steps, the method includes pre- and post-formulation functions, which are discussed in Chapter 4.

[11] The specialized & diversified DP is discussed in Chapter 6, Section 6.1.

facilitating the amendment of draft strategies; and (8) preserves and fosters the creative aspects of the strategy formulation process.

3.3   Step 1: The Identification of Relevant DPs

The identification of relevant DPs includes (a) the identification of core DPs and (b) the identification of strategy-specific DPs.[12]

a. The identification of core DPs

Executives or strategy teams can begin the DP identification process by including the five general core DPs,[13] which are discussed in Chapter 6, and can then include discipline-specific core DPs, such as the four manufacturing core DPs discussed in Chapter 7, the three marketing core DPs discussed in Chapter 8, or other discipline-specific core DPs.[14]

b. The identification of strategy-specific DPs

Following the identification of relevant core DPs, the executive or strategy team can identify or create strategy-specific DPs that reflect the policy goals and/or operational goals that are driving the formulation of the subject strategy.[15]

3.4   Step 2: Element Selection

In the second step, the executive or strategy team reviews each of the DPs that have been identified, and selects the element from each DP that they believe can (when combined with the elements that have been selected from other DPs) best contribute to achieving the subject policy goal or operational goal, by maximizing the use of resources and tactics.

In addition to selecting individual elements from a DP, in many cases executives and strategy teams can use both DP elements in a two-element hybrid.[16]

---

[12] These DP categories and terms are discussed in Chapter 5, Section 5.2.

[13] Types of core DPs are discussed in Chapter 5, Sections 5.2.1.

[14] Other discipline-specific core DPs are discussed in Chapter 5, Section 5.2.1.2.

[15] Strategy-specific DPs are discussed in Chapter 5, Section 5.2.2.

[16] DP hybrids are discussed in Chapter 5, Section 5.1.2.

3.4.1 Improving Element Selection

There are several ways to improve the selection of a strategy's elements. These include (a) avoiding non-selection, (b) avoiding wrong selection, (c) managing selection bias/habitual preference, (d) emphasizing situation specificity, and (e) formalizing element selection.

a. Avoiding non-selection

Non-selection occurs when an executive or strategy team fails to identify a DP that is relevant to the formulation of a strategy to achieve a policy or operational goal, and, therefore, does not select an element from that DP. The reason for non-selection may be that the executive or strategy team believes both elements in a DP are not relevant to the strategy being formulated, or because they are not familiar with the DP and its constituent elements. The non-selection of a necessary element can also be due to an intuitive or intentional desire to avoid or reduce a strategy's multiple-element complexity. This reason for failing to select needed elements is sometimes exacerbated by the *keep it simple* mantra, by the belief in silver-bullet solutions, and by single-element management fads.

b. Avoiding wrong selection

Wrong selection occurs when an executive or strategy team includes an unsuitable element from a dichotomous pair. The reason for wrong element selection may be because the executive or strategy team is not fully conversant with all aspects of the operational significance of both DP elements; and/or because they have selected a *default option*—which may be an option that is implied or mandated by a company's operating or managerial policies, or the selected element may be the industry-practice default option.

c. Managing selection bias/habitual preference

In many cases, wrong element selection occurs when an executive or strategy team is influenced by some form of selection bias, which may be due to their professional background in manufacturing, marketing, finance, human resources or other operational area; to their business ideological and/or philosophical beliefs; to the values, beliefs, and operating or managerial policies and/or practices of the company where they currently work or have previously worked; and/or to the zero-sum mindset.[17]

A common form of element-selection bias is habitual preference, which can drive the belief that one element of a DP is inherently better or worse than the other element, and can prevent an objective current-situation evaluation of the two elements from a DP.

Habitual preference frequently occurs when an experienced manager or executive has, following the repeated use of a particular element in the formulation of strategies, developed a strong prejudice in favor of or against that element. In some cases, an habitual preference is shared by managers and executives of a business unit, by managers and executives (and in some cases board members) of a company, or by most managers and executives in an industry or industry segment. In many cases, these habitual preferences only become apparent with the arrival of an out-of-business-unit, out-of-company, or out-of-industry participant in the strategy formulation process—or during strategy evaluation and approval.

d. Emphasizing situation specificity

Wrong selection during the element selection process, including wrong selection that is due to selection bias and habitual preference, can be offset by emphasizing the situation specificity of all strategies, by focusing on the current situation, and by focusing on the subject policy goal or operational goal that the current strategy is intended to achieve. The current situation may be similar to others that an executive or members of a strategy team have previously experienced or observed, but even in extremely similar situations, some aspects of the current situation are different. Also, past successes can be dangerous when they cause an executive or strategy team to not see critically important differences in ostensibly similar situations, which can result in them selecting an element from a DP that worked well in a previously successful strategy but will not be suitable or effective in the current strategy.

---

[17] The zero-sum mindset is discussed in Chapter 10, Section 10.3.1.

e. Formalizing element selection

In some cases, non-selection and wrong selection errors occur because the element selection process is not sufficiently disciplined and/or systematic. This can be addressed by adhering to the steps discussed in Section 3.3, and in earlier parts of this section.

3.4.2   The Formulation of Policy and Operational Goals

When boards of directors are engaged in the formulation of policy goals—and when boards of directors, or corporate or business-unit senior-level management, are engaged in the formulation of operational goals—they can use the same DP selection method that is discussed in this section. The multiple advantages of the DP selection method that apply to the formulation of corporate strategies and business-unit strategies also apply in the formulation of policy goals and operational goals.

3.5   Step 3: Element Weighting

The element-selection part of the strategy formulation process is followed by element weighting, where the terms *weight* and *weighting* refer to the relative emphasis that is allocated to each of the elements in a corporate or business-unit strategy.

3.5.1   The Weighting Process

During the weighting process, when one of the two elements in a DP is selected for use in a strategy, the executive or strategy team decides the weight that will be given to that element relative to the weight that will be given to the strategy's other elements. In situations where an executive or strategy team has chosen to include both elements in a DP hybrid, they decide (a) the weight that will be given to the DP hybrid relative to the weighting that is given to the strategy's other elements and (b) the relative weight that will be allocated to each of the elements that are included in the hybrid.[18]

---

[18] DP hybrids are discussed in Chapter 5, Section 5.1.2.

Weighting a strategy's constituent elements can be complex and difficult, because corporate and business-unit strategies can include a large number of elements, but also because of the large number of combinations and interactions between the elements, and the wide range of weightings that can be allocated to each of the elements. Also, because many of the elements in a strategy are interdependent, the decision to give one element more or less weight can change the relative weighting of other elements—which, in some cases, can change a strategy's focus and implementation effectiveness.

The relative weighting that is given to the elements in a strategy, and to the elements in a DP hybrid, can be seen as provisional, because the weighting of elements can be changed at different stages of strategy implementation, and during different phases of product, industry, and/or company life cycles.[19]

3.5.2   Subjective and Qualitative Aspects of Weighting

In strategy formulation, the weighting process can be influenced by multiple decision, design, and implementation factors. Determining what weight to allocate to each of the selected elements can also be complex and difficult because in many cases these decisions are not based on objective quantitative data, but are *value judgments* that must be based on an executive's subjective and qualitative knowledge and experience, and/or are based on the collective subjective and qualitative knowledge and experience of a strategy team.

The weighting of elements is often expressed using quantitative fractions or percentages, but the process for weighting a strategy's elements (for arriving at these quantitative fractions or percentages) is usually qualitative, and tends to be subjective. Even though the process may be largely qualitative and subjective, the results of the element-weighting part of the strategy formulation process must, however, be rationally and logically explainable and defensible—because the rationale for the weighing of the elements may have to be shared with levels of senior management, and, in the cases of corporate strategies, with the company's board.

---

[19] Product, industry, and company life cycles are discussed in Chapter 9.

3.5.3   *Weighting Bias*

Each of the element-selection bias factors discussed in Section 3.4.1.(c) can also be present during the element-weighting part of the strategy formulation process.

The possibility that an executive or strategy team may have to explain and/or defend a particular element weighting decision they have made during the weighting process can increase the emphasis on analytical and evaluation objectivity, which can be beneficial, because it can offset the tendency for weighting preferences to be affected by weighting bias.

3.6   Step 4: Element Configuration

In strategy formulation, the element-weighting part of the process is followed by element configuration, where the term *configuration* refers to the deliberate and intentional arrangement of a strategy's elements so they are at least mutually supportive and are at best synergistic. These two similar but distinct forms of configuration apply to all business strategies, including both corporate strategies and business-unit strategies.

There are two reasons for including and emphasizing the configuration requirement in the strategy formulation process. First, many plans (including many so-called strategies) include elements that are not mutually supportive or synergistic, and in some cases include elements that are mutually contradictory and/or countervailing. These contradictory/ countervailing element configurations can be seen historically in all types of strategies, from business and political strategies to international relations and military strategies. For example, the failure of the Iranian hostage rescue mission by the US military in 1980 (which led to the adoption of the 1986 Goldwater–Nichols Act by the US Congress) was attributed in large part to interservice rivalry that resulted in the use of strategies that included contradictory elements and countervailing element configurations.

Second, when a strategy's elements are structured in mutually supportive and synergistic configurations, this can result in significant plus-sum multiplier effects and can increase the strategy's performance, reliability, effectiveness, and sustainability.

3.6.1   *Mutually Supportive Combinations*

A characteristic that distinguished the multielement plans that were formulated by the *strategoi* in the ancient Greek city-states was that the plan's elements were chosen and configured so that they would be at least mutually supportive, and preferably would be synergistic.

In mutually supportive combinations, an added element (1) does not contradict, countervail, or diminish the effectiveness and/or functionality of any other element and (2) adds to and/or supports the quantitative or qualitative effectiveness and/or functionality of other elements.

3.6.2   *Synergistic Combinations*

The term *synergy* refers to a combination where the whole is equal to more than the sum of the parts. In some mutually supportive combinations, characteristic (2) from the previous paragraph is not simply additive, but produces a multiplier effect. In these cases, the degree to which an element contributes to the effectiveness and/or functionality of one or more other elements, or to the combined effectiveness of all of the other elements, is more than the sum of the effects of the individual elements.

3.7   Communication, Participation, and Amendment

The use of the DPs method can improve the formulation of corporate and business-unit strategies by facilitating communication, process participation, and the amendment of draft strategies.

3.7.1   *Communication*

The DPs method allows an executive or members of a strategy team to break a proposed strategy into its constituent elements, and to explain why they included each of the DPs from which they selected elements, and why they selected each element (and why they did not select the other element) from each of the selected DPs. Also, the method allows an executive or members of a strategy team to present a selected elements in comparative terms, by allowing them to show how and why—for this policy goal or operational goal, and for this strategy and this situation at this time—the selected element will be more suitable, more effective, more implementable, and/or in other ways will work better than the other DP element.

3.7.2   Participation and Amendment

The DPs method facilitates input and participation by a company's managers, executives, board members, and/or consultants, because it allows each of the constituent elements of a strategy to be addressed separately; and it allows each of the selected elements to be reviewed and possibly changed, rather than having to redo the strategy or have the strategy rejected.

3.8   Analyzing New and Existing Strategies

In addition to its use in the formulation of business strategies, the DPs method can be used by managers, executives, board members, and consultants to perform strategy analysis: when senior-level management and/or board members are engaged in a corporate or business-unit strategy evaluation and approval process; when executives and strategy teams are modifying corporate and business-unit strategies; and/or when managers, executives, board members and consultants are analyzing strategies being used by other companies.

When engaged in these functions, the analyst tries to identify the DPs that are being used in a corporate or business-unit strategy; tries to determine which element from each of those DPs is being used, and the relative weight that is being given to each element in each of these DPs (or, if the strategy includes the use of DP hybrids, to assess the relative weighting that is given to each of a hybrid's elements), and how the strategy's elements have been configured; and possibly tries to determine the rationale behind each of these DP-related choices, and the relative effectiveness of each of the selected elements from each of the DPs.

3.9   Modifying Existing Strategies

When an executive or strategy team is formulating a corporate or business-unit strategy, they are in many cases not beginning with a blank slate—because an underperforming or nonperforming strategy (or other plan, action, or response) already exists and is being implemented, or because there has been a change in the antecedent policy goal or operational goal—and in many cases it is not advisable and/or feasible to discard the existing strategy and start over. The most appropriate option in these situations is to analyze and evaluate the existing strategy, and then to engage in strategy modification, redesign, and/or repair. (In fact, more than one-third of my work in strategy formulation has included the modifying of existing strategies.)

When analyzing and/or evaluating an existing strategy, the DPs method can be used to identify all of the elements that are currently included in the strategy, and to then attempt to determine why each of the constituent elements was chosen, and why the other element from each of the DPs was not chosen; and to learn from the managers and executives who have been involved in the strategy's implementation about the observed beneficial or nonbeneficial effects of each of the strategy's constituent elements.

In some cases, the evaluation of a nonperforming, underperforming, or in some way unsuitable strategy can result in the identification of a necessary missing element, which can then be added to the existing strategy; or can identify one or more problematic elements, which (a) can be removed from the strategy, (b) can be removed and replaced with the other element from the DP, (c) can be retained, but given a different relative weighting, or (d) if it is part of a DP hybrid, can be given a different weighting relative to the other element in the hybrid.

CHAPTER 4

Pre- and Post-Formulation Functions

Contents

As discussed in Chapter 3, the primary functions in the DPs method are the identification of relevant DPs, and the selection, weighting, and configuration of elements. But because corporate and business-unit strategies are multielement plans for achieving one or more of an entity's goals, and because goals are the dependent variable that drives all strategy formulation—before an executive or strategy team can begin work on the identification of relevant DPs (and the selection of elements, and the weighting and configuration of the selected elements), they must first perform a critically important preformulation function: the identification, clarification, and confirmation of the strategy's antecedent policy goal or operational goal. This preformulation function is discussed in Section 4.1.

Also, after an executive or strategy team has completed the identification of relevant DPs, and the element selection, weighting, and configuration parts of the strategy formulation process (and before they present their strategy for approval, and/or before they begin strategy implementation) they must check their strategy for implementation feasibility and sustainability. These post-formulation functions are discussed in Sections 4.2 and 4.3.

4.1   Goal Confirmation

Before an executive or strategy team begins work on the identification of relevant DPs (and on element selection, weighting, and configuration) they must first identify, clarify, and confirm the antecedent policy goal or operational goal that the strategy is intended to achieve. The need to perform this preprocess goal-confirmation function may appear to be elementary, and it is, because it is impossible to begin formulating a strategy if you and/or your strategy team do not have a clear understanding of the goal that the strategy is intended to achieve. But although this may be elementary, the strategy formulation landscape is littered with less-than-successful or failed business strategies that were fundamentally flawed because the executive or team that was responsible for the strategy's formulation did not first identify, clarify, and confirm the antecedent policy goal or antecedent operational goal—or because their efforts to do this were offset by goal ambiguity.

4.1.1   Goal Ambiguity

Goal ambiguity (GA) can affect the identification, clarification, and confirmation of both policy goals and operational goals, and, therefore, the formulation of both corporate strategies and business-unit strategies. In most cases, GA only becomes apparent after a strategy has been implemented, when board members and/or senior-level management who were responsible for adopting or developing the goal indicate they believe the strategy was not suitable or successful. When this occurs, it often leads to the recognition that during the strategy formulation process there had been a lack of alignment between the *actual goal* that had been formulated by the company's board members, or (in the case of business-unit goals) by corporate or business-unit senior-level management, and the *assumed goal* that had been used as the dependent variable during strategy formulation process.

Goal ambiguity issues are often attributed to communication errors, but they can also be due to differences in goal perceptions by board members, or by executives at different levels of senior management; and/or by goal perception gaps between an entity's corporate and business-unit offices, or between an entity's home-country and host-country offices.

a. GA and corporate strategies

   In the case of corporate strategies, the chance of GA should be minimal, because most policy goals are contained in written resolutions that have been adopted by a company's board of directors. But the multiple "Whereas" paragraphs that preface many board resolutions can indicate that a policy goal resolution may not be adopted for a single reason, and can make the intended goal less focused and less clear. Also, the executive or strategy team members who were responsible for formulating a corporate strategy may not have seen the underlying board resolution until after they learn that some or all of the board members are not pleased with the strategy that was created to give effect to their resolution, and/or with the outcomes of the strategy's implementation.

b. GA and business-unit strategies

   In the case of business-unit strategies, the most common form of GA occurs when an operational goal is established by corporate senior-level management, and the strategies for achieving these operational goals are formulated and implemented by executives at the business-unit level. Differences in how the goal is seen by senior management at different levels in an organization often occurs during the formulation of response strategies, which are usually a type of business-unit strategy, and are discussed in Chapter 2, Section 2.3.1.2.

c. GA and corporate social responsibility

Executives and strategy teams are not responsible for the formulation of a company's corporate social responsibility (CSR) policies, because that responsibility lies with a company's board of directors. But executives and strategy teams are responsible for ensuring that the strategies they formulate, and the resources and tactics that are used in the implementation of these strategies, comply with their company's CSR policies. In some cases, GA is due to the absence of CSR policies, to inconsistencies in a company's CSR policies, or occurs when company or business-unit senior-level management put making the quarterly numbers ahead of compliance with their entity's CSR policies.

4.1.2   The Use of Goal Confirmation

Most well-managed companies have well-defined policies and policy goals. But even at these companies, an executive or strategy team must clarify and confirm the policy goal that is the purpose of the strategy they are formulating, because changes in policies and policy goals can be incremental and may not have been shared with all levels of management, or with executives in all of the company's business units. Also, identifying, clarifying, and confirming the antecedent policy goal(s) for a particular strategy can be difficult, because what looks like a corporate policy or business-unit policy may in fact be a policy position, an operating or managerial policy, or a policy slogan,[20] and corporate policies are sometimes inconsistent or contradictory.

The difficulties associated with identifying, clarifying, and confirming antecedent policies and policy goals notwithstanding, this preformulation part of the process is critical and essential, because it provides benchmarks that an executive or strategy team can use when they are identifying strategy-relevant DPs, selecting and weighting the elements from the dichotomous pairs, configuring the elements into mutually supportive

---

[20] Policy positions, operating or managerial policies, and policy slogans are discussed Chapter 2, Section 2.2.1.3.

and/or synergistic combinations, and checking the strategy for implementation feasibility and sustainability.

a. When modifying existing strategies

Identifying, clarifying, and confirming antecedent policies and policy goals is important when formulating new corporate strategies; but is especially important when fixing a strategy that is not working. No amount of modification, redesign, or repair can fix a strategy if there is uncertainty concerning its purpose, or if its purpose is not adequately grounded in a corporate policy goal or a business-unit operational goal.

b. When formulating response strategies

The need to identify, clarify, and confirm the antecedent policy goal or operational goal is often ignored by executives or strategy teams when they are engaged in the formulation of a response strategies,[21] because it is often assumed that the goal is self-evident: to remove the problem and return to the situation to the status quo ante that preceded the onset of the problem. But this assumption can be flawed, because the status quo ante included the condition(s) that caused the problem, or allowed the problem to occur. In some cases the problematic preexisting factor is structural or operational, but it may also be related to a policy goal or operational goal. In fact, some of my most difficult work in strategy formulation has been to convince senior-level management to address one or more antecedent causal factors, and not simply implement a strategy that would effect a return to the status quo ante. In some cases, this has led to having to put the strategy formulation process on hold, while changes were made to a structural or operational factor, or to an antecedent policy goal or operational goal.

c. When evaluating results

Antecedent policy goals and operational goals establish what a particular strategy is intended to achieve. Identifying, clarifying, and confirming antecedent policies, policy goals, and/or operational goals at the beginning of the process establishes criteria

---

[21] Response strategies are discussed in Section 2.3.1.2.

for evaluating the relative effectiveness of a strategy following its implementation.

d. When fixing goal-related errors

It may not be possible for executives and strategy teams who are responsible for the formulation of corporate strategies and business-unit strategies to eliminate the risk of goal-related errors during the strategy formulation process. These risks can, however, be minimized by adding a deliberate and formal preformulation process for identifying, clarifying, and confirming the antecedent goal(s) before work begins on the identification of DPs and the selection, weighting, and configuration of elements.

At some companies and/or business units, executives and strategy teams may be ragged for belaboring the goal identification, clarification, and confirmation preprocess parts of strategy formulation. But if this occurs, it is a small price to pay for reducing the risks and related adverse effects that can accrue from not taking seriously the need for these preprocess functions.

4.2   Implementation Feasibility

A mouse trapped in a corner by a cat called to a strategy mouse, "What should I do?"

The strategy mouse replied, "Bark like a dog."

The trapped mouse called back, "How do I bark like a dog?"

The strategy mouse replied, "My area is strategy formulation, not implementation."

4.2.1   Checking for Feasibility

Implementation is a sine qua non of strategy: If a strategy is not implementable, for whatever reason, it is worthless. There are several ways to check a strategy for implementation feasibility, which include checking for the availability of resources; checking for constituency compatibility; and running implementation scenarios.

4.2.1.1   The Availability of Resources

In the above trapped-mouse sketch, the tactic proffered by the strategy mouse was worthless, because the trapped mouse lacked the necessary physical resources and methods resources it would have needed to bark like a dog. The absurdity of this sketch notwithstanding, the implementation of strategies can require access to and use of many different tangible, intangible, internal, and external resources—and the absence of one or more necessary resources can result in a strategy being unimplementable, or can compromise or limit effective implementation.

In many cases, strategy implementation has been prevented or impeded due to a missing or nonavailable resource, which was overlooked during strategy formulation because it was either intangible or thought to be insignificant. Although it may not be possible to eliminate the resource-availability risk that is associated with strategy implementation, this risk can be minimized by using a checklist that includes the physical resources, financial resources, human resources, intellectual property resources, relationship resources, reputation resources, and methods resources categories that are discussed in Chapter 2, Section 2.4.1.

4.2.1.2   Constituency Compatibility

A second way to check a strategy for implementation feasibility is to check it for constituency and stakeholder compatibility. The origins of the term *constituency* are political: A constituency is a group of voters on whom a representative or official is dependent to be elected and/or to stay in office. Since the late 1970s, the term has also been used to refer to individuals and groups that can affect a company's survival, success, and sustainability.

A company's constituencies can include bankers (and other institutional lenders), bond holders, customers, distributors, employees, end users, the company's host communities (from which the company draws its employees and where the company has offices and/or factories), the media, national and local governments and government agencies (including regulators and taxing authorities), retailers, shareholders, shippers and carriers, suppliers, and trade unions. Because the relative importance of an entity's constituencies depends on many factors (which include the size and type of the company or business unit, the industry, the location, and the situation) constituency identification and weighting is entity and situation specific, and the constituencies in the previous sentence are listed in alphabetical order and are not prioritized.

For publicly listed companies, constituencies also include financial analysts, financial journalists, the government entities that regulate publicly listed companies, and the stock exchange(s) where a company is listed. Some constituency groups are referred to as *stakeholders*, because they hold an interest or stake in the company's survival, success, and sustainability. The terms constituency and stakeholders are often used interchangeably, but they are not synonymous. The term constituency is broader than the term stakeholders, because it includes individuals and groups that do not have a direct stake in the company. For example, legislators, regulators, and environmental groups are in a position to influence the survival and success of a company, but they do not have a stake in the company.

The values, beliefs, and behaviors of constituencies can affect an entity's survival, success, and/or sustainability—but constituencies can also be critical variables in the success or failure of business strategies. Because of this, implementation feasibility checking should include the identification of constituencies and/or constituency subgroups that could affect a strategy's implementation; the weighting and prioritizing of each constituency and/or constituency subgroup for its possible effect at different stages of the strategy's implementation; and checking each of the strategy's elements in terms of its possible effects on each constituency and/or constituency subgroup. In some cases, this part of the strategy formulation process can lead an executive or strategy team to reassess the suitability and/or weighting of elements from one or more DPs, to change the weighting that is allocated to an element, to change the weighting of the elements in a DP hybrid, or even to change their choice of elements from one or more DPs.

4.2.1.3   Running Scenarios

A third way to check a strategy for implementation feasibility is to run a series of implementation scenarios. The term *scenario* refers to the outline of the plot of a play, or, more generally, of an imagined situation. When used in forecasting, as it is used here, the term refers to a postulated sequence of events. When running an implementation scenario, an executive or strategy team imagines each of the steps that will be involved in the implementation of the proposed strategy, and looks for possible events that could prevent or limit its full and effective implementation.

Implementation scenario runs can be used to ensure (1) that the strategy addresses all aspects of the antecedent policy or operational goal; (2) that all aspects of the strategy are consistent with relevant corporate and/or business-unit policies; (3) that the company has (or can acquire the use of) the physical resources, financial resources, human resources, intellectual property resources, relationship resources, reputation resources, and methods resources needed to implement the strategy; (4) that all of the strategy's tactical elements comply with relevant legal and ethical standards, and with the entity's CSR policies;[22] and (5) that the strategy's implementation is constituency compatible.

When running feasibility scenarios, it is important that executives and strategy teams focus on identifying possible factors that could cause the strategy not to work. This can be difficult for some executives and members of strategy teams who, by training and/or temperament, prefer to look at the positive aspects of plans they have developed. Aggressive downside analysis is, however, a necessary part of effective feasibility evaluation.

Aggressive downside analysis also prepares executives or strategy teams to discuss a strategy's weaknesses, which may be necessary if they need to present the strategy to colleagues, senior-level management, individual board members, and/or their company's board.

4.2.2   Issue Manageability

If the feasibility analysis of a proposed strategy is thorough, comprehensive, and aggressive, it will usually identify at least one, and in some cases several, implementation feasibility issues. The first step in addressing

---

[22] Strategy and CSR policies are discussed in Section 4.1.1.(c).

implementation feasibility issues is to determine if each issue is manageable or non-manageable.

a. Manageable issues

In this context, a *manageable issue* is a possible implementation problem that can be fixed by in some way modifying the strategy. In some cases, the strategic element that has been identified as the cause of a possible implementation feasibility issue can be removed from the strategy without seriously adversely affecting the strategy's potential effectiveness. In other cases, a feasibility issue can be fixed by changing the choice of element from a DP, such as switching from build to buy (or from buy to build)[23] or from alone to allied (or from allied to alone);[24] by changing the weighting of the elements in the strategy, or changing the weighting of the elements in a DP hybrid; or by replacing an element with an element from a different dichotomous pair.

b. Non-manageable issues

A *non-manageable* issue can be defined as a possible implementation problem that cannot be fixed by modifying the strategy. If implementing a strategy would cause the company to violate ethical standards or break the law, this should result in the implementation problem being classified as non-manageable. If a strategy would violate a corporate policy, or would require the use of unavailable resources, the implementation issue can be classified as non-manageable; but this classification should be provisional, because in some cases it may be possible to have a corporate policy amended, and there may be a way to acquire (or to acquire the use of) the necessary resources, which would mean that the issue is in fact manageable.

4.2.3   Premature Rejection

All proposed strategies should be subjected to implementation feasibility evaluation, but an excessive emphasis on feasibility at the early stages of the

---

[23] The build & buy DP is discussed in Chapter 6, Section 6.3.

[24] The alone & allied DP is discussed in Chapter 6, Section 6.4.

strategy formulation process can be counterproductive—because it can result in the premature rejection of a strategy that is flawed, but may be fixable and usable. Because of this, seemingly unimplementable strategies should not be discarded, but instead should be *shelved*, in case the implementation issue can be solved, or in case some part of the strategy can be used.

a. Prima facie flawed strategies

Because some implementation issues that appear to be non-manageable are in fact manageable, it is important that executives and strategy teams who engage in strategy formulation (and senior-level management who engage in strategy evaluation and strategy approval) not be too quick to classify an implementation issue as non-manageable.

b. The devil's advocate

Premature rejection can also occur at the very early stages of strategy formulation, when a strategy-team member or senior-level executive raises implementation feasibility objections. In some cases, the antagonist may believe the company or business unit should not waste time and other resources on the development of a strategy that is fundamentally flawed, or they may believe that playing the devil's advocate is part of their job description. Whatever the reason, ill-timed devil's advocacy can result in the discontinuation of work on a nascent and potentially suitable strategy.

c. The feasibility self-gambit

A worse case of premature rejection occurs when an executive or strategy team discontinues work on a potentially suitable strategy because they cannot see an immediate solution to an implementation issue. The feasibility self-gambit often occurs when an implementation issue falls outside the executive's or strategy team's areas of expertise, or because a required implementation-issue function would fall outside the scope of their authority.

4.3   Implementation Sustainability

Checking strategies for implementation feasibility is necessary but not sufficient, because executives and strategy teams must also check to ensure that the proposed strategy will, when implemented, satisfy the strategy sustainability criteria that are implied or stated in the subject policy goal or operational goal. The term *strategy sustainability* refers to the potential of a strategy to continue to be effective over time.

One of the inherent differences between tactics and strategy is that in many cases tactics are not a sustained activity: Their purpose is to perform an immediate short-term function, and they are not intended to be, or expected to be, sustainable. An important characteristic of strategies, however, is that, following their implementation, they are expected not only to perform their intended function—but to continue to perform that function.

4.3.1 Sustainability Myopia

There is a tendency for executives and strategy teams to ignore strategy sustainability, which can be due to the proclivity for tactics, which is discussed in Chapter 2, Section 2.5.4, and/or to the emphasis that many companies place on short-term results. At the macroeconomic level, Lester Thurow and other political economists have detailed how the emphasis on making the quarterly numbers adversely affects national competitiveness. But this short-term emphasis can also adversely affect the survival, success, and sustainability of individual companies and business units, because it motivates executives to apply their abilities and energies, and their entity's resources and tactics, to the generation of current-quarter revenues—rather than to the formulation and implementation of corporate and business-unit strategies that are designed to achieve corporate growth and sustainability.

4.3.2 Improving Implementation Sustainability

The critical factor that most improves the post-implementation sustainability of corporate and business-unit strategies is, ironically, not in how a strategy is implemented, but how the subject strategy was formulated. The key to strategy sustainability lies in the degree to which executives and strategy teams consider and emphasize sustainability when they engage in the identification of relevant DPs, the selection of elements from each of the identified DPs, and the weighting and configuration of the selected elements—and if during each of these parts of the strategy formulation process they give special attention to factors that can have a positive or negative effect on a strategy's sustainability. These factors can include the availability, choice, and use of the company's physical resources, financial resources, human resources, intellectual property resources, relationship resources, and methods resources; the development and use of the company's core competencies; company (or business unit), industry, and product life-cycle positions;[25] their entity's host business environment; and the values, beliefs, and priorities of the company's internal and external constituencies.

A second method for improving the implementation sustainability of some corporate and business-unit strategies is to employ plus-sum strategies. As discussed in Chapter 10, Section 10.4, plus-sum strategies are highly sustainable. Because plus-sum strategies benefit all parties, all parties are motivated to adopt a plus-sum mindset when making strategy-related decisions; to engage in sustainability-enhancing behaviors and actions; and to avoid decisions, behaviors, or actions that could adversely affect the strategy's continued implementation and effectiveness. The sustainability of all strategies, and especially plus-sum strategies, can also be enhanced through the use of plus-sum structures and plus-sum environments.[26]

---

[25] Life-cycle positions are discussed in Chapter 9.
[26] Plus-sum structures and environments are discussed in Chapter 10, Section 10.4.2.

CHAPTER 5

The Dichotomous Pairs

Contents

The DPs method, and the use of the DPs method in the formulation of corporate and business-unit strategies, are discussed in Chapter 3.

This chapter discussed the composition of dichotomous pairs, including the relative superiority of DP elements and the use of DP hybrids; and DP categories, which include general core DPs, discipline-specific core DPs, and strategy-specific DPs.

Twelve core DPs, and their use in the formulation of corporate and business-unit strategies, are discussed in Chapters 6, 7, and 8.

5.1 The Composition of DPs

Each of the DPs used in the formulation of business strategies includes two distinct elements that are seen as possible functional alternatives. The two elements in a DP can be opposites from within a generic classification, or can be alternatives from different generic classifications.

Opposites from within generic classifications include the specialized & diversified, vertical integration & vertical separation, and allied & alone

DPs discussed in Chapter 6; the insource & outsource, manual & automated, and domestic & international DPs discussed in Chapter 7; and the production orientation & market orientation, and primary demand & secondary demand DPs discussed in Chapter 8. Alternatives from different generic classifications include the build & buy and profits & growth DPs discussed in Chapter 6; the scale & flexibility DP discussed in Chapter 7; and the differentiation & segmentation DP discussed in Chapter 8.

5.1.1   The Relative Superiority of Elements

Neither element in any of the DPs is inherently superior to the other element. Because all strategies are situation specific, the superiority of an element from a DP is situation specific—and depends on the goal the strategy is intended to achieve, on other elements that are being used in the formulation of the strategy, and on the strategy's stage of implementation. In some situations, one element from a DP will be more suitable for use in a particular corporate or business-unit strategy; in another situation, the other element will be more suitable. When the situation changes, the relative suitability of a DP's elements may change. The situation suitability of a DP element can also be influenced by product, industry, and company life-cycle phases.[27] Where both DP elements are used in a hybrid, a change in the situation may require a change in relative weighting of the hybrid's constituent elements.

5.1.2   DP Hybrids

As discussed in Chapter 3, Section 3.4, the elements in each DP are dichotomous, but they are not mutually exclusive; and the use of one element does not prevent the concurrent use of the other element. When executives and strategy teams are formulating corporate strategies or business-unit strategies, they frequently combine both DP elements in a hybrid.

---

[27] Life-cycle phases are discussed in Chapter 9.

Element weighting, which is discussed in Chapter 3, Section 3.5.1, refers to the weight that is given to a DP hybrid relative to the weighting that is given to the strategy's other elements—but also refers to the weighting that is given to each of the elements that are included in a hybrid, which can range from both of a DP hybrid's constituent elements being given approximately equal weighting (50:50), to them being given extremely disproportionate weighting (90:10). The relative weighting of a DP hybrid's constituent elements, like the relative weight given to each element in a strategy, can be changed at different stages of strategy implementation, and during different phases of industry, corporate, and/or product life cycles.

5.2   DP Categories

The DPs used in the formulation of corporate and business-unit strategies can be grouped into two primary categories: (1) core DPs and (2) strategy-specific DPs.

5.2.1   Core DPs

The term *core dichotomy*, or *core dichotomous pair* refers to a frequently and widely used DP that is seen as performing a central, important, and in some cases indispensable role in the formulation of corporate and business-unit strategies. Core DPs can be grouped into two subcategories: (1) general core DPs and (2) discipline-specific core DPs.

5.2.1.1   General Core DPs

General core DPs can be used in the formulation of all (or almost all) corporate and business-unit strategies; and include the five DPs discussed in Chapter 6: specialized & diversified, vertical integration & separation, build & buy, alone & allied, and profits & growth.

It is important to note that although this list of five general core DPs has been time tested in a wide range of situations, is not intended to be exhaustive—and executives and strategy teams at some entities may need to create additional general core DPs for their entity, for their entity's AOD, and/or for their entity's life-cycle position.

5.2.1.2   Discipline-Specific Core DPs

Discipline-specific core DPs can be used in the formulation of all (or almost all) corporate and business-unit strategies within a particular discipline or functional area of business (such as manufacturing or marketing). Discipline-specific core DPs include the four manufacturing core DPs discussed in Chapter 7 (scale & flexibility, outsource & insource, manual & automated, and domestic & international) and the three marketing core DPs discussed in Chapter 8 (production & market orientation, primary & secondary demand, and differentiation & segmentation).

Other discipline-specific core DPs include, inter alia, human resources management core DPs, accounting and financial management core DPs, supply chain management core DPs, information systems management core DPs, and international business core DPs. Executives and strategy teams that are engaged in the formulation of corporate and business-unit strategies in these and other business disciplines create sets of discipline-specific core DPs, which are similar to the sets of manufacturing core DPs and marketing core DPs that are included in Chapters 7 and 8. As discussed in Section 5.2.2, an executive or strategy team can choose to add a frequently used strategy-specific DP to their list of discipline-specific core DPs.

5.2.2   Strategy-Specific DPs

Strategy-specific DPs are dichotomous pairs that are driven by the strategy's antecedent policy goals or operational goals, and are created by an executive or strategy team during the formulation of a corporate or business-unit strategy.

The core DPs discussed in the previous sections are critically important parts of the strategy formulation process; but all strategies are situation specific, and a strategy's situation specificity is driven by the strategy's antecedent policy goal or operational goal. Because of this, when executives or strategy teams are formulating corporate or business-unit strategies, they must identify or create strategy-specific DPs that reflect the policy goals and/or operational goals that are driving the formulation of the subject strategy.

5.2.3   *Category Overlap*

There can in some cases be an overlap between the two primary DP categories, when a core DP (either a general core DP or a discipline-specific core DP) reflects the policy goals and/or operational goals that are driving the formulation of the subject strategy, and function as a strategy-specific DP.

Also, when an executive or strategy team sees that they are using a strategy-specific DP in all (or almost all) strategies for a particular functional discipline, they can choose to add this DP to their list of discipline-specific core DPs.

PART 3
Core DPs

CHAPTER 6

General Core DPs

Contents

The term *core dichotomy*, or *core dichotomous pair*, refers to a frequently and widely used DP that is seen as performing a central, important, and in some cases indispensable role in the formulation of corporate and business-unit strategies. The five core DPs discussed in this chapter are called *general core DPs* (as distinct from *discipline-specific core DPs*), because they can be used in the formulation of all (or almost all) corporate and business-unit strategies.[28]

When executives or strategy teams are formulating corporate or business-unit strategies, they can begin by selecting elements from the five general core DPs discussed in this chapter. Then, depending on the type of strategy being formulated, they can select elements from the manufacturing core DPs discussed in Chapter 7 or the marketing core DPs discussed in Chapter 8, or from other discipline-specific core DPs.[29] They must then identify or create strategy-specific DPs that reflect the policy goals and/or operational goals that are driving the formulation of the subject strategy, and select elements from those strategy-specific DPs.[30]

6.1   Specialized & Diversified

In most cases, when companies come into existence they select the specialized element from this DP, and perform a narrowly defined group of functions, such as manufacturing and marketing beer or selling books online. Over time, companies can remain relatively specialized, or they can choose to diversify.

6.1.1   Specialized

Selecting the specialized element allows a company to focus its energies and resources on a narrow industry AOD, which facilitates the development and acquisition of a specialized set of resources, including core competencies; allows a company to maximize the use of those resources;

---

[28] Core DPs are discussed in Chapter 5, Section 5.2.1. General core DPs are discussed in Chapter 5, Section 5.2.1.1.

[29] Discipline-specific core DPs are discussed in Chapter 5, Section 5.2.1.2.

[30] Strategy-specific DPs are discussed in Chapter 5, Section 5.2.2.

and allows a company to maximize the use of its experience, reputation, and relationships in a specific industry sector, and with specific products. Specialization allows the world's largest beer company, AB InBev, to focus on the manufacture and marketing of 630 brands of beer in 150 countries. Specialization has allowed the BYD Auto business unit at BYD to focus on the design, development, manufacture, and marketing of electric vehicles—and to become the world's largest EV company.

The specialized element from this DP can cover a wide area, and some entities that choose the specialized element are more specialized than others. For example, Intel, Samsung, Texas Instruments, and other integrated device manufacturers (IDMs) that design, develop, and manufacture semiconductors (using their own fabrication plants) can be seen as being more broadly specialized. Taiwan Semiconductor Manufacturing Company (TSMC), however, can be seen as being more narrowly specialized. Since TSMC was founded in 1987, by Morris Chung, it has been a *pure-play foundry*, performing semiconductor manufacturing for fabless semiconductor companies, including Apple, ARM, Broadcom, Marvell, MediaTek, Nvidia, and Qualcomm—and for some IDMs, including Intel and Texas Instruments.

In corporate governance, the reason for establishing separate business units is in many cases done to create financial and accounting firewalls between profit centers. But breaking a corporation into business units also facilitates specialization. For example, even though BYD manufactures the batteries used in the manufacture of its EVs, these batteries are designed, developed, and manufactured by the company's FinDreams Battery business unit; whereas the EVs are designed, developed, and manufactured by its BYD Auto business unit—which allows each of these business units to specialize on its own industry AOD.

In manufacturing, specialization allows a company to focus its resources on the acquisition and utilization of specialized production equipment and specialized core competencies, to develop the ability to produce a limited range of products efficiently and at a high level of quality, to maximize economies of scale, to carry less raw material and parts inventory, and to hire employees who have specialized skills and abilities. In marketing, specialization allows a company to pursue penetration strategies, rather than skimming strategies. Because specialization results in a company having a relatively narrow range of products, it can allow a company to carry less finished products inventory, to establish a reputation for expertise in a specialized area, and to hire employees who have specialized skills and abilities.

Selecting the specialization element from this DP can, however, have several downsides. Because specialization restricts a company or business unit to a single industry, or industry segment or subsegment, it can limit growth—and can be unsuitable for entities in low-growth and/or low-profit industries, and for entities in mature industries. If a company or business-unit is operating in a cyclical industry or industry segment or subsegment, the use of the specialized element can increase its exposure to industry downturns.

6.1.2 Diversified

Selecting the diversified element from this DP allows a company to expand its AOD, and to pursue opportunities in different segments of the same industry or in different industries, which can allow an entity to avoid many of the downsides of specialization. Selecting the diversification element can facilitate growth; and can reduce a company's vulnerability to industry downturns, improve a company's financial performance, and in some cases can rejuvenate mature companies in mature industries.

A disadvantage of selecting this element can be that diversification spreads an entity's resources over an increased number of operational areas—which can result in the dilution of a company's physical resources, financial resources, human resources, intellectual property resources, relationship resources, reputation resources, and methods resources. Also, because diversification can move a company outside its industry AOD, it can move a company outside its principal areas of expertise, which can dilute the company's core competencies. When carried to extremes, diversification can make a company a conglomeration of unrelated activities and can adversely affect investor interest.

6.1.2.1   Related and Unrelated Diversification

All diversification can be classified as either related or unrelated. When a company expands its AOD by diversifying into an operational area where it can use its core competencies, it is engaged in related diversification. When Amazon diversified into selling things other than books (which expanded its AOD by extending the use of its selling-things-on-line core competencies), it was engaged in related diversification.

When Amazon acquired Alexa Internet in 1999; created its Amazon Web Services (AWS) business unit in 2001 (which since 2016 has generated more than half of Amazon's corporate profits); and in 2023 became the primary cloud provider for Anthropic, and took an equity position in this AI start-up—none of these diversifications were related to Amazon's selling-things-online AOD. But because each of these diversifications was directly related to Amazon's online IT core competencies, they were all related diversification.

When a company diversifies into an operational area where it cannot use its core competencies, it is engaged in unrelated diversification. When Amazon purchased Whole Foods Market in 2017, it was engaged in unrelated diversification.

In some cases, what appears to be unrelated diversification is, in fact, related. This is because related diversification can be either technical or operational. The diversification by General Motors into car financing in 1919 was technically unrelated. Car financing is part of the financial services industry, which is a long way from GM's motor vehicle industry AOD. But this diversification by GM was operationally related to its core AOD, because GMAC facilitates the sale of motor vehicles made and marketed by GM. When Amazon invested in the development, manufacture, and marketing of the Kindle, which was released in 2007, it was technically not related to Amazon's online book-selling AOD; but because the Kindle is a product for reading Kindle Edition formatted books, it was operationally related.

If a company's business units are engaged in AODs that cover a wide range of unrelated industries, the company is referred to as a *conglomerate*. When carried to extremes, unrelated diversification produces the conglomerates that proliferated in the 1960s, which included business units that were often totally unrelated. For example, during Harold Geneen's tenure as CEO of International Telephone and Telegraph (ITT), the company acquired or merged with more than 300 companies, including Avis Car Rental in 1965, Continental Baking (and its Wonder Bread manufacturing and marketing operations) and Sheraton Hotels in 1968, and Hartford Insurance in 1970.

The conglomerate concept is based on the belief that good managers can manage anything, that industry specialization limits the pursuit of profits and growth, and that diversification reduces an entity's exposure to industry downturns. Also, the senior-level management and boards at conglomerates have argued that they have not moved outside their area of core competency, because their defining core competency is their ability to concurrently and effectively manage widely disparate entities and operations. Many conglomerates have, however, performed poorly when compared to more specialized companies, and (with some notable exceptions, which include Berkshire Hathaway, China Resources Group, Reliance Industries, Samsung, and the Tata Group) the conglomerate concept has lost favor and credibility with most CEOs, company boards, and individual and institutional investors.

6.1.2.2   Horizontal and Vertical Diversification

The diversified element from the specialized & diversified DP takes two primary forms: horizontal and vertical. An entity is engaged in horizontal diversification when it diversifies into a AOD function that does not come before or after its present scope of operations. Horizontal diversification can be either related or unrelated.

A company or business unit is engaged in vertical diversification when it diversifies into an AOD function that comes before or after their present scope of operations. All vertical diversification is related diversification. Vertical diversification, which is also called vertical integration, is discussed in Section 6.2.

6.1.3   Application

The two elements from the specialized & diversified DP define a continuum. It is possible to identify a company's position on the continuum, and to identify if a company has moved on the continuum, and, if it has, in which direction it has moved.

Pepsi is close to the middle of the continuum. If Pepsi had followed a more specialized strategy, it would have focused more of its resources on its cola products, and its cola wars with Coca-Cola. But Pepsi diversified into other soft drinks, and diversified into non-drink areas. Beginning in 1965, it merged with a snack foods company, acquired other snack foods companies, and created a snack foods division; between 1977 and 1986, it acquired Pizza Hut and KFC, and created a restaurants division. Each of these actions moved Pepsi closer to the diversified end of the continuum. When Pepsi spun off its restaurants division into Yum Brands, this moved Pepsi back toward the specialized end of the continuum.

Since IBM started adding AI and chip making divisions in 2010, and since it purchased Manta Software Inc. in 2023, it has been moving closer to the diversified end of the continuum.

When Amazon's AOD was limited to selling books online, it was at the specialized end of the continuum. When it started selling other products online, it moved marginally toward the diversified end of the continuum. When Amazon acquired Alexa Internet, and created AWS; when it invested in the development, manufacture, and marketing of the Kindle; when it purchased Whole Foods Market; and when it took an equity position in AI start-up Anthropic, it moved significantly closer to the diversified end of the continuum.

6.2   Vertical Integration & Separation

All diversification can be defined as being either vertical or horizontal.[31] Vertical diversification is also referred to as *vertical integration*, and can be either backward or forward. Vertical separation limits an entity's area of domain, and relies on other entities to perform functions that precede or follow their AOD operations.

6.2.1   Vertical Integration

Vertical integration is a form of diversification, which expands an entity's AOD by including a business process or activity that comes either before or

---

[31] See Section 6.1.2.2.

after an entity's present scope of operations. Because the added process or activity precedes or follows the entity's present scope of operations, vertical integration is always related diversification. Vertical integration can be classified as either (1) backward vertical integration or (2) forward vertical integration.

6.2.1.1   Backward Vertical Integration

Backward integration expands a company's AOD to include a process or activity that precedes its present scope of operations. When General Motors established an EV battery laboratory in Michigan in 2021, and in 2024 entered into a joint venture with Lithium Americas to develop the Thacker Pass lithium mine in Nevada, to source lithium for EV batteries, GM was engaging in backward vertical integration.

Backward vertical integration can be used to reduce dependency on external suppliers and supply chains, and to increase control of the availability of a material, component, or service. Companies often cite quality control as the reason for engaging in backward vertical integration, especially if the quality of the particular material or component is critical to the company's competitive advantage. Another frequently cited reason for engaging in backward vertical integration is to control costs. If a company is its own supplier, it avoids the possibility of being coerced into paying a supplier's price. Backward vertical integration can help a company to improve its profitability by controlling the cost of a material, component, or service.

Some backward vertical integration decissions are not driven by a past or present availability, quality, and/or cost problem—but reflect a concern by senior-level management that there could be a problem in one or more of these areas in the future. In these cases, a company removes or reduces uncertainty related to a future situation by using backward vertical integration to secure control of the future availability, quality, and cost of a material, component, or service.

6.2.1.2   Forward Vertical Integration.

Forward vertical integration expands a company's AOD to include a process or activity that follows its present scope of operations. The founder of

Kodak, George Eastman, began doing research (which he first patented in 1879); and then forward vertically integrated into manufacturing and marketing Kodak photographic film and camera products; and then forward vertically integrated into retailing these products through a chain of Kodak stores.

In 2003, BYD acquired Xi'an Qinchuan Automobile, which was a small manufacturer of gasoline-powered cars. This acquisition by BYD appeared to be totally unrelated diversification, because at the time BYD was the world's largest manufacturer of NiCd rechargeable batteries, which are used in phones and other electronic products. But because the reason for making this acquisition was to secure a plant, production line, investment and manufacturing permits, and other motor vehicle manufacturing resources that BYD would need to design, develop, manufacture, and market battery-powered vehicles—this acquisition by BYD was related diversification, and, more specifically, was forward vertical integration. BYD Auto introduced its first plug-in hybrid EV in 2008; introduced its first battery electric vehicle in 2009; and discontinued the manufacture of gasoline-only cars in 2022. In 2023, BYD became the world's largest manufacturer of electric vehicles.

As discussed in Section 6.2.1.1, the most cited reasons for engaging in backward vertical integration are the need for control; but the need for control can also be a factor that drives a company's decision to forward vertically integrate into downstream operations. These downstream operations may include subsequent manufacturing processes, or one or more marketing functions, such as distribution or retailing.

In 2022, BYD announced it had placed orders for eight roll-on roll-off ships, with individual carrying capacities of between 7,000 and 9,200 cars or trucks, and a collective annual shipping capacity of more than one million vehicles. When the company took delivery of the first of these ships in 2024, and began international shipping operations, it was again engaged in forward vertical integration, which provided the company's BYD Auto business unit with more control over its international distribution, and provided a sustainable competitive advantage for its international market penetration strategy.

6.2.1.3   Backward and Forward Vertical Integration

Backward and/or forward vertical integration can be used to expand a company's AOD; facilitate growth; reduce dependency on third parties; increase control of the availability, quality, and cost of a material, component, or service; improve profitability; and reduce future uncertainty. Both backward and forward vertical integration can also be used to reduce or remove a company's dependency on third parties that provide the company with a material, component, or service; or that distribute or retail the company's products. In most cases, the purpose of a vertical integration strategy is to reduce, rather than remove, third-party dependency.

The benefits of vertical integration notwithstanding, it can have several downsides. Because it is a form of diversification, vertical integration can dilute a company's core competencies, and can take a company or business unit outside its areas of expertise and outside its AOD. An operational downside of vertical integration is that, in terms of supply chain management, managers and executives are captive of their sibling business units and are no longer free to choose their source of materials, components, and/or services.

6.2.2   Vertical Separation

Vertical separation limits a company's or business unit's area of domain, and relies on other entities to perform functions that precede or follow the company's or business unit's present AOD operations. Using the vertical separation element provides options and flexibility, it uses suppliers as a source of innovation and competitive advantage, and it facilitates specialization.

The freedom to choose and change the provider of a material, component, and/or service is one of the primary benefits of a free-market economy. If one supplier does not deliver a material, component, and/or service at a competitive price, or if there are problems related to availability or quality, a company or business unit using the vertically separated element is able to turn to alternative suppliers. This benefit has increased, and will continue to increase, with globalization.

Competition between suppliers can be a source of innovation and a way of controlling costs. A characteristic of the Japanese industrial system is the *keiretsu*, which is a group of companies that includes a large manufacturer, banks, and an extended family of suppliers. The large manufacturer is linked to the suppliers by long-term supply agreements, equity interests and long-term loans, the sharing of technology, and the sharing of development costs. Toyota, which since 2008 has been the world's largest motor vehicle company, uses its *keiretsu* (which includes about 800 companies) to remain vertically separated from its suppliers, to encourage innovation, and to ensure supply chain quality and price competition.

Vertical separation respects the principle of the division of labor, avoids the dilution of core competencies,[32] and provides many of the other benefits of specialization.[33] But the use of the vertical separation element can make a company dependent on third parties for the availability of parts, components, and services; in some cases can make it difficult to control the quality and cost of parts and components; and it can limit growth.

6.2.3   Application

Because most companies perform two or more sequential functions in some area of their operations, most companies are to some degree vertically integrated. But even if two companies are in the same industry, and make and market the same type of product, they may give different weight to the use of the vertical integration element. General Motors, which manufactures far fewer cars than Toyota, has five times the number of employees, manufactures many more of its own components, and is more vertically integrated. Toyota relies on outside suppliers that are part of its *keiretsu*, and is less vertically integrated.

The elements from this DP can be seen as forming a continuum, and executives and strategy teams can use hybrids that include both elements.

6.3   Build & Buy

Most companies and business units come into existence because they are built. They initially build a workforce, physical facilities, core

---

[32] Core competencies are discussed in Chapter 2, Section 2.4.4.

[33] Specialization is discussed in Section 6.1.1.

competencies, products, markets, brand loyalty, and the other factors that contribute to their survival and success; and a company or business unit can grow by continuing to build in all of these areas. A business entity can, however, also grow by buying other companies; buying business units from other companies; and/or buying physical facilities, products, intellectual property, sourcing and distribution networks, and other resources from other companies.

6.3.1 Build

The build element can provide fit, cost, and feasibility benefits. The literal meaning of the verb *to fit* is to join two things together to form a whole; but the term is also used as an adjective to indicate that a thing is suitable for an intended purpose. The fit advantage of building means a company can design and build exactly what is needed. When using the build element, a company can build a new production plant in the optimal geographic location, which can have exactly the production line and equipment that is needed; or can build a workforce that is designed specifically for its intended purpose. Using the build element increases the probability that each operative element will perform its intended function and will be compatible with the entity's culture, operating norms, and procedures.

Building can cost less than buying, because a company or business unit can use and add to its current physical resources and human resources. Expanding sales by increasing the number of sales people and/ or distributors can be less expensive than buying another company or buying a business unit from another company. Expanding manufacturing capacity or diversifying into a new area of manufacturing by building a new production plant, and hiring additional workers and supervisors, can cost less than buying another company or buying a business unit from another company. Also, in some cases building can be more feasible than buying, because the cost of building can be spread over an extended period of time, and the build element is often chosen by companies that do not have the financial resources to buy; and sometimes the build element is the only available option because the desired addition cannot be purchased.

The build element can, however, have several limitations:

1. A company may not have the physical resources, financial resources, human resources, intellectual property resources, relationship resources, reputation resources, and/or methods resources needed to use the build element. For example, a company may not have the needed core competencies to plan, execute, and operate the desired addition.
2. The build element can be slow. It takes time to build a factory, develop and install new manufacturing equipment, hire and train employees, design and develop products, build market share, and build product and/or company reputations. Because building can be slow, selecting the build element can incur a high opportunity cost: the delay caused by using the build element may mean the new investment will take too long to produce a significant return, and/or could cause a company to miss a window of opportunity.
3. When a company uses the build element, executives and strategy teams must base decisions on future unknown variables; they must make decisions based on projections of future industry and market conditions, the ability of suppliers to provide materials and components, and customer demand for a new product. Executives and strategy teams must also anticipate problems that could be encountered, which can include manufacturing and quality problems, distribution problems, and the possible future reaction by competitors to the company's diversification into a new industry segment or to it introducing a new product. Also, the situation can change during the time it takes to implement a build strategy.

6.3.2 Buy

In some cases, a company can simultaneously achieve high levels of profits and growth[34] by buying one or more other companies, or by buying business units from other companies. The buy element can (1) include needed resources, (2) be fast, (3) reduce risk, and (4) facilitate the extension of a company's area(s) of domain.

---

[34] The profits & growth DP is discussed in Section 6.5.

The buy element can facilitate the acquisition of physical plant and equipment, manufacturing capacity, skilled and experienced employees, intellectual property, core competencies and other methods resources, technology, products and/or product lines, distribution networks, markets and/or additional market share, company names, product brands, and company and product reputations. AB InBev became the world's largest beer company when the Artois brewery in Leuven, Belgium, used the buy element to acquire breweries in Belgium and the Netherlands in the 1960s, 1970s, and 1980s—and to acquire AmBev in Brazil in 1999, Anheuser-Busch in the US in 2008, and SABMiller in the UK and South Africa in 2016. In 2005, Lenovo used the buy element to acquire IBM's personal computer operations, and the right to use the IBM brand for five years, which trebled Lenovo's size, and made it the world's third-largest PC company. In 2010, Tesla used the buy element to acquire the NUMMI plant, in Fremont CA, from Toyota; and, in 2017, Rivian Automotive used the buy element to acquire the Chrysler-Mitsubishi plant, in Norman IL, from Mitsubishi.

When buying a company or business unit, the buy element can reduce risk, because senior-level management can evaluate the tangible and intangible assets being acquired; can evaluate the entity's operational, managerial, and financial condition; and can assess related company, industry, and product life-cycle positions.[35] Even when a company is buying another company that has product, operational, and/or financial problems (as when GM, Suzuki, and SAIC purchased the assets of Daewoo Motors, after Daewoo had declared bankruptcy) the risks can be more known and more manageable than if the company were using the build element.

The buy element can be used to change a company's industry area of domain. When Jack Welch became chairman and CEO of General Electric (GE), he drew a Venn diagram that defined the industries and industry segments where GE would operate, set the parameters of GE's industry AOD policy, and drove GE's divestiture and acquisition strategy. Welch sold business units that fell outside the circles of his Venn diagram, and used the proceeds from the sale of those business units, together with GE stock, to buy companies that fell within the Venn diagram's circles.

---

[35] Life-cycle positions are discussed in Chapter 9, Section 9.2.

This realignment of GE's industry AOD was the most systematic and extensive ever undertaken by a major multinational corporation—and was only possible because of GE's aggressive use of the buy element.

In 1999, Amazon began the diversification of its AOD into web services and AI, by buying Alexa Internet, a web traffic analysis company. In 2003, BYD used the buy element to acquire Xi'an Qinchuan Automobile, and to diversify its AOD from the manufacture and marketing of NiCd rechargeable batteries to the manufacture and marketing of cars, buses, and trucks.[36]

Companies and their business units can also use the buy element to extend their geographical AOD, by providing additional geographical coverage in their home country, or by acquiring new or additional foreign direct investment (FDI) and operating presence in a host country. For example, when GM, Suzuki, and SAIC[37] used the buy element to acquire 66.7 percent of the assets of Daewoo Motors in South Korea, in 2001, (and began operations as GM Daewoo in 2002) this increased GM's geographical AOD in Asia.

For publicly listed companies, buying can have significant feasibility benefits, and can have financial and accounting advantages, because the purchase can be paid for (in whole or in part) with company shares. When Lenovo acquired IBM's PC division, it used a combination of company stock, cash, and the assumption of debt.

The disadvantages of the buy element are related to availability, suitability, and feasibility. In some cases the buy element cannot be used because there is no suitable company or business unit available to be purchased. If there is a company or business unit available for purchase, the price may be high, it may not be in a suitable location, it may not be a suitable size or have suitable facilities, and there may be concerns related to the caliber of its employees or the compatibility of its manufacturing facilities, products, and/or corporate culture. There may also be concerns about acquiring contingent liability, and a company may not have the financial or equity resources needed to use the buy element.

---

[36] This acquisition by BYD is discussed in Section 6.2.1.2.
[37] GM's relationship with SAIC is discussed in Section 6.4.2.

6.3.3 Application

The elements from the build & buy DP can be used in a wide range of DP hybrids. In most cases, it is impossible to pursue a pure build strategy—because building requires materials and labor, and a company needs to buy the necessary physical materials and human resources with which to do the building. For example, when implementing a manufacturing strategy, a company buys components for use in the product it will build; when a company builds additional productive capacity, it usually buys the production machinery.

In the company life cycle,[38] the build element usually precedes the use of the buy element. Companies and business units in the introductory and early growth phases of their life cycles usually have limited resources with which to buy core competencies, technology, products, or market share from other companies, or to buy companies or business units. The buy element is usually not feasible until a company has accumulated financial reserves and/or has become a publicly listed company. There are, however, exceptions to this generalization, and some companies in the early growth phase of their life cycle have used the buy element.

6.4   Alone & Allied

In the past, executives and strategy teams formulated corporate and business-unit strategies that included one of the elements from the build & buy DP, or included both elements in a DP hybrid. But the expanded use of strategic alliances has, in some cases, made the build & buy DP a false dichotomy—because SAs provide a third option that allows entities to choose to build, buy, or ally.

6.4.1 Alone

There is a wide preference among executives and strategy teams for the alone element from this DP. Some of the reasons for this preference are managerial and/or operational, and some are based on philosophical beliefs.

---

[38] Company life cycles are discussed in Chapter 9, Section 9.3.

The most frequently cited reason for preferring the alone element is managerial and operational: that it provides control. Shared control, which is a central element of alliances, is antithetical to the traditional role of executives and senior-level management who are recognized and rewarded for their ability to formulate and implement strategies, make operational decisions, and actively manage an entity's financial, physical, and human resources. Even at entity's that have decentralized managerial philosophies and structures, senior-level management is accountable, not only for the financial performance of each business unit but also for the quality and safety of each unit's products, for the ethical behavior of the unit's managers, and for the unit's treatment of employees and the physical environment.

Managerial accountability is accompanied by the need, or perceived need, for operational control. The alone element provides control of policy goals, priorities, and corporate culture; control of the use of assets (including control of intellectual property, and control of the use of funds); and control of the decision-making process. Using the alone element also has the operational advantage that it avoids the downsides of alliances. The alone element avoids having to find alliance partners and to negotiate alliance agreements; it avoids potential conflicts related to policy goals, values, beliefs, priorities, and corporate cultures; it simplifies decision-making; and it saves time. And the alone element avoids a company's exposure to partner risk.[39]

The preference for the alone element from this DP (and an aversion to the allied element) can also be philosophical. Many executives and strategy teams believe that merging complementary interests, sharing privileged information, and engaging in intimate collaboration and cooperation contradict traditional business norms. These executives and strategy teams tend to see alliances as unnatural business phenomena, and prefer the clarity of the arm's-length, competitive, adversarial, and zero-sum nature of the alone element.

In the case of US executives and strategy teams, these beliefs and preferences may be in part because, according to Hofstede's Country Individualism Index, the United States is the most individualistic society in the

---

[39] Partner risk is discussed in Chapter 10, Section 10.4.1.3.

world, and alliances are a collectivist concept. This possibility is supported by the extensive and successful use of strategic alliances by Japanese companies, and Japan is a collectivist society.

In the current business environment, however, SAs are a widely used mechanism for achieving and maintaining competitive advantage. If a company or business unit limits its options to the use of the elements from the build & buy DP, this can adversely affect the entity's ability to achieve and maintain competitive advantage—which can adversely affect earnings, growth, and sustainability.

6.4.2   Allied

When used in the formulation of corporate and business-unit strategies, the allied element is generally referred to as a strategic alliance.[40] SAs are less-than-arm's-length relationships[41] that can provide the cost, fit, and feasibility advantages of building; and the speed, risk reduction, resources acquisition, and AOD extension advantages of buying. As discussed in Chapter 10, Section 10.4.1, they are called *strategic alliances*, rather than alliances, to indicate that their purpose is to achieve one or more of an entity's policy goals or operational goals.

Strategic alliances are based on the belief that, by working together and combining their resources, business entities can achieve results that would not be possible if they acted alone, and can produce mutual benefits and synergies that are equal to more than the sum of their individual contributions.[42] The less-than-arm's-length structure of SA relationships, and the collaboration and cooperation between SA partners, can facilitate the transfer of management, manufacturing, and marketing technologies; can provide access to the physical resources, financial resources, human resources, intellectual property resources, relationship resources, reputation resources, and methods resources that are discussed in Chapter 2, Section 2.4; can satisfy regulatory requirements; can facilitate

---

[40] Strategic alliances are also discussed in Chapter 10, Section 10.4.1.
[41] Less-than-arm's-length relationships are discussed in Chapter 10, Section 10.4.1.1.
[42] Synergy is discussed in Chapter 3, Section 3.6.2.

and expedite operations; and can facilitate the evaluation of merger and acquisition opportunities.

In 1997, GM wanted to enter the car manufacturing industry in China, but was unable to use either element from the build & buy DP, because, at that time, foreign direct investment in the auto industry was restricted to a 50 percent ownership in an equity joint venture with a Chinese-funded company.[43] GM complied with this FDI requirement by entering into a strategic alliance with SAIC, a Shanghai state-owned enterprise. In 1999, SAIC-GM began assembling Buick Regal sedans and Buick GL8 minivans; and, by 2003, GM's sales from SAIC-GM were second to its sales in the US. The SA introduced Cadillacs in 2004, and Chevrolets in 2005; it began exporting cars to South America in 2006; and in 2016 it began exporting the Buick Envision to the United States.

In 2020, Amazon created its Climate Pledge business unit, which entered into SAs with BETA Technologies, CarbonCure Technologies, Redwood Materials, Rivian Automotive, Turntide Technologies, and ZeroAvia, for the purpose of developing decarbonizing/sustainable technologies, products, and services. The SA with Rivian included a $700-million equity investment by Amazon, and covered the design, development, and manufacture of EV delivery vans and EV charging stations. By 2025, Amazon was using more than 20,000 Rivian EV delivery vans in the US, and 300 in Germany.

In 2017, Xiaomi Automobile Technology, an EV start-up in China, entered into an SA with Beijing Automotive Group (BAIC), which allowed Xiaomi to use BAIC's manufacturing permits and facilities, and to design, develop, manufacture, and market cars while securing its own manufacturing permits and while building of its own factories.

Strategic alliances also provide a way for companies and business units to explore merger and acquisition possibilities. Because SAs allow the senior-level management of both entities to learn firsthand about the other entity, they are a proven *try-before-you-buy* mechanism that can

---

[43] In 2018, this restriction was removed for FDI in the manufacture of fully electric and plug-in hybrid vehicles. In 2022, the restriction was removed for all auto-industry FDI.

reduce the risks and concerns related to buying another company or business unit, or being bought by another company or business unit.

6.4.3   Application

As discussed at the beginning of Section 6.4.1, many executives and strategy teams dislike the allied element for managerial, operational, and philosophical reasons. But selecting the allied element can also have other downsides. (1) Using the allied element can be inconvenient; it takes time to find an alliance partner and to negotiate an alliance, and operating in an alliance can be complicated and time-consuming. For example, all major decisions in a strategic alliance must be considered and decided by both partners, who may have very different policy goals, values, beliefs, and priorities—and different ways of evaluating situations and making decisions. Because of this, decisions that normally take days can, in SAs, take months. (2) Many SAs have serious operational problems, and many are short lived. (3) All SAs come with an inescapable downside called *partner risk*, which is the exposure of an SA partner to the possibility of opportunistic behavior by the other partner.[44]

6.5   Profits & Growth

The formulation of most corporate and business-unit strategies is driven or influenced by one or both of the elements from the profits & growth dichotomy.

6.5.1   Profits

Historically, the US business model has emphasized the profits element. At publicly listed companies, profits can add to shareholder wealth directly, through the distribution of dividends, and indirectly by increasing the value of the company's shares. In some cases, the emphasis on the profits element has been driven by operational requirements. Executives and strategy teams at publicly listed companies, and especially at large

---

[44] Partner risk is discussed in Chapter 10, Section 10.4.1.3.

multinational corporations, frequently emphasize profits because products and projects are held to strict earnings and profitability timetables and earnings/profitability hurdle-rates.

Executives and strategy teams at privately held companies also tend to emphasize the profits element, because (1) positive cash flow is a critical factor in the survival and success of privately held companies and (2) they need profits to fund their growth, and/or need profits as a prerequisite to raising additional debt or equity capital. These executives or strategy teams may prefer to focus primarily on growth, but they pursue profits because emphasizing profits improves cash flow, and profits can be a necessary precondition for growth.

But the need to make the quarterly numbers, and/or to produce positive cash flow, can motivate executives or strategy teams to focus on profits—rather than formulating and implementing strategies that address the growth aspects of corporate or business-unit goals.

Also, the need to make the quarterly numbers and/or produce positive cash flow can cause executives or strategy teams to limit investment in R&D, product line expansion, product development, manufacturing equipment and methods, marketing and distribution, and can motivate senior-level management to implement downsizing and apply other cost-cutting measures. These actions can have a positive effect on profits and cash flow, but can adversely affect an entity's productivity, performance, and growth.

6.5.2 Growth

The term *growth* can be applied to an increase in sales (measured either in revenues or the number of units sold), market share, product range, core competencies, the size of workforce, and/or the number of manufacturing plants, retail stores, or other physical resources. The term growth can also be applied to an increase in profits, but in this DP the term refers to the sales, revenues, and/or the market share meanings listed in the previous sentence.

Historically, the Japanese business model has emphasized growth. In surveys of Japanese companies, most members of senior-level management did not include share price in their top ten priorities. These executives said their primary concerns were for the welfare of the company's or business unit's employees and suppliers, for their entity's reputation with its customers, for its continued growth, and for maintaining and/or increasing market share.

At publicly listed companies, the growth element can add to shareholder wealth by increasing the value of the company's shares. Investors are influenced by profits, but they are also influenced by growth and the potential for future growth; and emphasizing the growth element in strategy formulation can maximize the use of a company's or business unit's physical resources, financial resources, human resources, intellectual property resources, relationship resources, reputation resources, and/or methods resources.

6.5.3 Application

When confronted with the choice between profits and growth, many senior-level executives and board members say they want both. It is not surprising, therefore, that business strategies frequently include a profits & growth DP hybrid.

The use of a profits & growth hybrid when formulating corporate and business-unit strategies does not, however, avoid decisions related to the use of the profits and growth elements, because executives and strategy teams must decide what weight to allocate to each of the DP hybrid's constituent elements. Also, in some cases it can be difficult or impossible for a company or business unit to simultaneously emphasize both elements, because emphasizing profits can adversely limit growth, and emphasizing growth can adversely affect profits.

In recent years, there has been a convergence in the preferences at US and Japanese companies for the elements of this DP. Some Japanese companies have increased their emphasis on profits and stock price, some US companies have become more focused on growth and market share, and some US companies have pursued what were previously Japanese strategies. For example, for years after creating Amazon, Jeffrey Bezos said there would be no profits for the foreseeable future, which allowed him to focus on growth, to reinvest earnings, and to avoid being pressured by investors to produce profits. It took eight years before the company declared a profit, but by then the company's annual revenues were in excess of $5 billion.

The de-emphasizing or deferral of the profits element can also be seen at DeepSeek, the AI developer founded in China, in 2023, by Liang Wenfeng. Following the release of its DeepSeek Coder in 2023 and DeepSeek-V2 in 2024, the company released its DeepSeek chatbot for iOS and Android in 2025, which within weeks had displaced ChatGPT from OpenAI as the most downloaded AI freeware app. In a 2024 interview, Liang said, "In this wave, our starting point is not to take advantage of the opportunity to make a quick profit, but rather to reach the technical frontier and drive the development of the entire ecosystem."[45]

The choice of the profits or growth element from this DP (and the relative weighting of the elements in a profits & growth hybrid) can be influenced by product, industry, and company/business-unit life-cycle positions.[46]

---

[45] Schneider, Jason, et al. *China Talk*. November 27, 2024.
[46] Life-cycle positions are discussed in Chapter 9.

CHAPTER 7

Manufacturing Core DPs

Contents

The term *discipline-specific core dichotomous pair* refers to a frequently and widely used DP that is seen as performing a central, important, and in some cases indispensable role in the formulation of corporate and business-unit strategies—within a particular discipline or functional area of business (such as manufacturing or marketing).[47]

When executives and strategy teams are engaged in the formulation of manufacturing strategies, they can select elements from the five general core DPs discussed in Chapter 6, and from the four discipline-specific manufacturing core DPs discussed in this chapter. As with the formulation of all corporate and business-unit strategies, the executive or strategy team must then identify or create strategy-specific DPs that reflect the policy goals and/or operational goals that are driving the formulation of the subject strategy, and select elements from those strategy-specific DPs.[48]

7.1   Scale & Flexibility

The scale & flexibility DP includes some of the characteristics from the specialized & diversified core dichotomy, which is discussed in Chapter 6, Section 6.1, but the elements from the scale & flexibility DP are used primarily in the formulation of manufacturing strategies.

7.1.1   Scale

Since the beginning of the industrial revolution, the scale element from this DP has dominated manufacturing mentality, manufacturing strategy, and manufacturing operations. The scale element can be used to provide economies of scale, to increase purchasing bargaining power, to facilitate the division of labor, and to improve product quality.

a. Economies of scale
    The scale element from this DP can reduce the cost of the product being manufactured. The term *economies of scale* refers to cost reductions that can result from the manufacture of a large number of identical (or, in some cases, similar) units. Economies of scale are achieved by distributing the fixed costs of production over an

---

[47] Discipline-specific core DPs are discussed in Chapter 5, Section 5.2.1.2.
[48] Strategy-specific DPs are discussed in Chapter 5, Section 5.2.2.

increased number of identical units, which reduces the fixed costs per unit of the product being manufactured. The term *fixed costs* refers to costs that do not change when there is a change in the number of units being produced, and can be either direct or indirect. Indirect fixed costs can include the cost to buy, build, or lease factories and assembly plants; R&D costs; and administrative and overhead costs, which do not change when there is a change in the number of units being produced. Direct fixed costs can include the cost to design a product (and other product-specific R&D costs); the cost to buy, build, or lease production equipment, machinery, and tools needed to manufacture a particular product; the cost to design, develop, and test a production line; the cost to train workers to make a product; and/or the cost to test a product. The economies of scale benefit can be especially important for the survival, success, and sustainability of companies or business units in capital intensive industries that have high fixed costs.

b. Purchasing bargaining power

The scale element can increase a company's bargaining power when purchasing materials, and especially when purchasing parts and components or when a company wants a supplier to design, develop, and/or manufacture specialized parts and components. When a company orders a larger number of materials or parts, the supplier can offer a lower price per unit, because it will benefit from economies of scale.[49]

c. The division of labor

The scale element can help to reduce production costs by facilitating the division of labor. Adam Smith showed in his *Pin Factory* example that the "division and combination of different operations" can greatly increase productive output, reduce costs, and improve quality when manufacturing a large number of relatively small and simple products. But, as Henry Ford showed during the first quarter of the twentieth century, it is the manufacture of a large number of a relatively large and complex product that provides the greatest opportunity for a manufacturer to break tasks down into

---

[49] In this chapter, most references to companies also apply to business units.

increasingly specialized increments, and to apply division of labor principles and practices. Also, it is in large-scale manufacturing operations where the division of labor can result in the greatest cost, quality, and productivity benefits.

d. Product quality

The scale element can justify a high level of investment in the design, development, and/or acquisition of specialized single-purpose production equipment and/or machinery, and can justify the cost of developing and/or acquiring specialized tooling and processes, the development and/or acquiring of specialized core competencies, and hiring and/or training a workforce with specialized skills. Each of these factors can reduce the production cost per unit. These factors can, both individually and collectively, increase the quality of what is produced.

7.1.2   Flexibility

The economies, purchasing power, division of labor, and quality benefits of the scale element have for generations motivated senior-level management to develop a strong preference for the scale element. But the scale element can have significant disadvantages. In many cases, large-scale production lines that are designed to make one product cannot be used to make a different product. In some cases, production lines are designed to make more than one product, but reconfiguring these production lines can be slow and expensive.

The scale element can cause a company to limit the number of different products it makes, to limit the number of different models of a product, and/or to limit (or not offer) optional product features, and can prevent a company from modifying a product to satisfy individual customer requirements. Henry Ford's fixation with the scale element caused him to make only one product, and to offer it only in one color, which in 1931 led Ford to lose its sales-volume market-share leadership position to General Motors.

The term *flexibility* in this dichotomy refers to the ability of a manufacturing production line and/or process to make different products, to make different models of the same product, to vary the characteristics or features of a product, and/or in some cases to customize each unit produced. Flexibility also refers to the ease with which a manufacturing production line and/or process can be reconfigured to make different products or models, or to customize products or models. The flexibility element can provide manufacturers with production, marketing, and globalization benefits.

a. Production advantages

The flexibility element and the use of *flexible manufacturing systems* (FMSs) can increase or decrease production volumes in response to market demand, seasonal demand, and/or to stockpile inventory; speed product and model changeovers; reduce cycle times, tooling costs, and downtime; and can allow a larger mix of products. FMSs can also require shorter lead times and can reduce materials and parts inventories. These production advantages led Toyota to develop its Flexible Body Line and Global Body Line assembly systems, which it says resulted in a 70 percent reduction in the time required to complete a major model change, and a 50 percent reduction in the cost to add or switch models, in initial investment, in assembly line footprint size, in energy usage and carbon dioxide emissions, and in maintenance costs.

b. The marketing advantages

The flexibility element can also provide marketing advantages, by allowing a company to increase the number of different products and/or models it makes on the same production line, to modify products to satisfy individual customer requirements, to offer consumers a wider range of products, and to reduce order-to-delivery times.

c. The globalization advantages

The flexibility element allows companies to adjust manufacturing output to meet market and international supply chain management demand, to improve plant productivity, to achieve intraplant and interplant production flexibility, and to tailor production to satisfy customers preferences; and allows manufacturers to maximize the global flexibility of the company's manufacturing resources.

The primary downside of the flexibility element is that it can prevent an entity from achieving and maximizing the economies of scale benefits. This downside of the flexibility element has been offset, at some entities, by their emphasis on continuous improvement, which has resulted in the development of methods resources that combine economies of scale with flexible/intelligent/agile manufacturing.

7.1.3 Application

Although all strategies are situation specific, the preference for a DP element can, in some cases, be company and/or country specific. For example, in the auto industry, the preference for the economies of scale element was made famous by Henry Ford in the US; the preference for the flexibility element was pioneered and made famous by Toyota in Japan. Henry Ford saw change as the enemy of economies of scale. Toyota sees change and continuous improvement as keys to achieving higher quality and lower costs, and Toyota and many other Japanese companies include continuous improvement as one of the three key elements of TQM. Henry Ford's plants and processes were designed to remove the need for production-line workers to make decisions. Toyota's manufacturing environment empowers production-line teams to create and implement improvements to production-line processes, and employee empowerment is another key element of Total Quality Management.

Globalization and the emphasis on continuous improvement in Japan, the US, Europe, and more recently China, has resulted in the development of methods resources that combine economies of scale and flexible manufacturing. These multidimensional hybrids use high-capacity, high-speed data processing hardware and software to achieve shorter lead times, low-cost customization, small lot size, fast change-over times, lower average cost per unit, and consistently high quality. In Japan these initiatives are called *intelligent manufacturing*, in the US they are usually called *agile manufacturing*.

7.2   Outsource & Insource

One of the most fundamental DPs in the formulation of manufacturing strategies is "should we do it ourselves, or should we have it done by someone else."

7.2.1   Outsource

When a company uses another company to manufacture a part, component, or product—or to perform a manufacturing process instead of performing that process itself—the company is using the outsource element.

In manufacturing, the outsource element allows a company to specialize, to use other companies' core competencies, to reduce costs, and to increase their productive capacity. The outsource element can also be used to save time, support innovation, and improve manufacturing flexibility. In China, Volkswagen outsources the manufacture of parts to 500 component partners, who supply its Shanghai VW and FAW VW joint ventures, which on average results in the outsourcing of two-thirds of the components used in each vehicle. VW's component partners increase the productive capacity of Shanghai VW and FAW VW, reduce their direct and indirect costs, allow them to specialize, add to their core competencies, save them time, contribute to their innovation, and improve their manufacturing flexibility.

a. Increasing productive capacity

When a company needs additional manufacturing capacity, the outsource element provides a means of using the plant, equipment, and employees of another company or of several other companies.

b. Reducing costs

Because outsourcing uses the plant, equipment, and personnel of another company, or a number of other companies, it reduces the manufacturer's working capital requirements. When Toyota outsources the design, development, and manufacture of parts and components to members of its *keiretsu*, it is the *keiretsu* members who must make the investment in R&D, part and component design, buildings, machinery, and human resources.

c. Facilitating specialization

The outsource element facilitates specialization,[50] because a manufacturer can outsource those production functions that are outside its immediate AOD. In manufacturing, specialization allows a company to focus its resources on the acquisition and utilization of specialized production equipment, to maximize economies of scale, to carry less raw material and parts inventory, and to hire employees who have specialized skills and abilities.

Outsourcing allows a company to focus on a narrow set of core competencies that are related directly to its core business. For example, outsourcing allows auto industry companies to focus on core competencies related to the design, development, manufacture, assembly, and testing of a vehicle's major components—and on core competencies related to vehicle marketing, distribution, and service—and allows companies to avoid having to develop core competencies related to the design, development, manufacture, assembly, and testing of thousands of individual parts, components, and component packages.

d. Saving time

Outsourcing can save time. It takes time for a manufacturer to build or retrofit a plant, purchase production equipment, and hire and train a workforce to make a part, component, or product, or to perform a manufacturing process. When a company outsources a part, component, product, or process to a company that already has the necessary plant, machinery, and highly skilled workforce, it avoids the time delays in acquiring each of those necessary elements of production. If the manufacturer outsources to a company with the necessary core competencies, it can achieve further time savings by avoiding or reducing learning-curve delays.

e. Supporting innovation

Toyota and other Japanese motor vehicle companies use members of their *keiretsu* to design, develop, and manufacture parts and

---

[50] Specialization is discussed in Chapter 6, Section 6.2.1.

components for their vehicle production lines. This system uses at least two suppliers for each item, which (in addition to reducing single-source dependency) encourages quality and price competition, and generates innovative product and production initiatives. One reason Texas Instruments outsources part of its semiconductor manufacturing to Taiwan Semiconductor Manufacturing Company, which is the world's largest pure-play foundry, is to take advantage of TSMC's specialized core competencies, lower labor costs, and innovative capabilities.

f. Providing flexibility

In situations that are uncertain, and in industries that are characterized by change, the outsource element can be used to provide flexibility. When a company is unable to determine the size of a proposed production line, because it is impossible to determine the potential demand for a product, or when it is unclear whether the company should invest in additional productive capacity and/or set up a dedicated production line for a new product, the company can use the outsource element to delay these decisions until it has better data.

7.2.2   Insource

The outsource element can provide many tactical, strategic, and operational advantages. The primary downside of the outsource element relates to the loss of control. Companies that use the outsource element can encounter quality control problems, delivery delay problems, price escalations, or some other dissatisfaction with availability, quality, performance, and/or price. Also, using the outsource element can be inconvenient and time-consuming.

The reason many companies backward integrate[51] is because their senior-level executives are unsatisfied with the quality, availability, suitability, and/or price of a material, part, or service that is available from suppliers or contract manufacturers. When a company manufactures a part, component, or product itself—or performs a manufacturing process

---

[51] Backward integration is discussed Chapter 6, Section 6.2.1.1.

rather than having it done by another company—the company is using the insource element. For example, VW's joint ventures in China outsource two-thirds of their components, whereas BYD insources three-quarters of the components for its Seal electric hatchback sedan. The advantages of the insource element can include, inter alia, control, cost, and convenience.

a. Control

When a company insources the manufacture of a product, it controls the quality of the materials and workmanship, the scheduling and completion date, who has access to the intellectual property in the product, and the core competencies used in the manufacturing process. Midea, which is the world's largest producer of major appliances—which include heating, ventilation, and air conditioning products, home appliances, and robotics and other automation products that the company markets under multiple brands—has for years been progressively implementing an insource strategy. This has included the backward integrating into the manufacture of refrigeration compressors, which has allowed Midea to include new technology in the manufacture of its air conditioners, gives the company direct control over the quality of this key component of its air conditioners, and provides better control over on-time delivery and component costs.

b. Cost

Insourcing can also allow a company to better control the cost of production. If a company already has the plant and equipment needed to make a particular product, insourcing can achieve economies of scale,[52] amortize the capital cost of plant and equipment, and reduce the cost per unit. Insourcing can also reduce costs by avoiding the costs of transporting materials, parts, and/or products to and from another company; and insourcing avoids a company or business unit having to contribute to another company's overhead and profits.

---

[52] Economies of scale is discussed in Section 7.1.1.

c. Convenience

The insource element can also be more convenient, because it avoids the logistical and administrative hassles of having to deal with second and third parties.

Relying on the insource element can, however, be restrictive and can adversely affect a company's competitive advantage.

7.2.3 Application

The elements from this DP offer a large number of combinations, which change over time as product, industry, and company life-cycle positions change, as the business environment changes, and/or as other situational factors change.

a. Situation specificity

A company that does not have the necessary specialized core competencies or the specialized manufacturing equipment to make a part for a new product may initially use the outsource element. When sales volumes justify the acquisition of the new core competencies and specialized manufacturing equipment, the company may change to the insource element.

Or the order can be reversed. A company may begin by using the insource element, then change to the outsource element to increase productive capacity, cut costs, access core competencies and innovation, and/or improve manufacturing flexibility. For example, in 1969, Advanced Micro Devices (AMD) began by using the insource element and manufactured its semiconductor chips at AMD fabrication plants—and its founding chairman and CEO, Jerry Sanders, famously boasted that "real men have fabs." But in 2009, AMD spun off its fabrication division into GlobalFoundries, and since then AMD has outsourced the manufacture of its chips.

b. Evolution and evaluation

Historically, companies have preferred the insource element, and many senior-level executives and board members share Jerry Sanders' bias against outsourcing. But advanced managerial thinking and the use of SAs[53] has meant that most executives and strategy teams are now able to objectively evaluate both elements. The choice between the elements from this DP is, as with all strategy formulation, company and situation specific, but some of the most commonly used criteria include operational factors (such as productive capacity, speed, the availability of core competencies, and flexibility), life-cycle positions, cost–benefit calculations, and strategic sensitivity.

c. Strategic sensitivity

For many years, the criterion that dominated decisions concerning the outsourcing of manufacturing functions was strategic sensitivity; which was defined as parts, components, products, or processes that provided a company with competitive advantage. A widely held rule-of-thumb said that a company should retain control of, and not outsource, the design, development, and manufacture of strategically sensitive parts, components, products, or processes. Also, it would have been unthinkable to outsource any of these strategically sensitive manufacturing functions to a present or potential competitor. The evolution and expansion of global outsourcing practices, the growth in the number and size of the companies that provide contract manufacturing, and the cost–benefit criterion have become dominant variables—and have caused many companies to reduce the weight they give to the strategic sensitivity criterion. Because of this change in weighting, strategically sensitive parts, components, products, and processes are now frequently outsourced, even to a competitor.

d. Area of domain

When senior-level management is deciding if they should outsource part of their company's financial and accounting services, legal services, human resources services, data center operations, information technology functions, and payroll functions, they can base their decision primarily on cost–benefit calculations. But deciding whether or not to outsource one or more manufacturing functions

---

[53] Strategic alliances are discussed in Chapter 6, Section 6.4.2; and in Chapter 10, Section 10.4.1.

can be more complex, because when a company outsources these functions, it may be outsourcing a part of its AOD. The de-emphasis of the strategic sensitivity criterion and the emphasis on cost-related criteria have caused some companies in some industries, such as Nvidia Corporation in the AI industry, to adjust their industry AOD; to focus on product research, product development, and marketing; and to outsource their manufacturing functions.

7.3   Manual & Automated

An issue that has been at the center of manufacturing operations since the invention of the cotton gin by Eli Whitney, in 1793, has been the use of manual and automated manufacturing methods. The term automated manufacturing methods, as used here, includes both mechanization (which includes industrial robots) and AI. When executives and strategy teams are formulating manufacturing strategies, this perennial issue is reflected in the choice of elements from the manual & automated DP.

The manual & automated dichotomous pair is included here as a manufacturing DP, because both elements from this DP have historically been associated with manufacturing. As indicated by some of the examples in this section, the manual & automated DP also applies to nonmanufacturing areas and situations; but the issues covered in most of those examples also apply to manufacturing.

This is the only DP discussed in this book where one element is generally favored by workers and organized labor, and the other element is generally preferred by operations management, senior-level management, and company boards.

7.3.1   Automation and Organized Labor

Since the beginnings of automation, workers have generally seen industrial machines in terms of the number of employees they replace, and, therefore, as a threat to their employment; which has driven the widespread worker opposition to automation, and has increased the probability of unionization by the most exposed workers. A 2020 MIT News article titled "How many jobs do robots really replace?" cites US automation research "showing that each robot added to the workforce has the effect of replacing 3.3 jobs."[54]

During the early years of the industrial revolution, workers protested against the use of automation by striking and through sabotage—by throwing their wooden clogs (*sabots*) into textile-making machines. In the current era, automation is frequently the critical issue that has driven labor actions, such as the 2024 strike by the members of the International Longshoremen's Association (ILA) against US Maritime Alliance (USMX), which operates ports on the East Coast and Gulf Coast of the US, and the ILA's demand that USMX agree to not implement automated technology, and especially automated technology that could eliminate dockworker jobs, at ports over the life of their labor contract.

The perceived threat by workers and organized labor is exacerbated by the increasing use of industrial robots (which globally now number more than one million on automotive production lines, and about three million across all industries), which a 2019 report by Oxford Economics estimated will replace 8.5 percent of the global manufacturing workforce by 2030.

Adding to this perceived employment threat from industrial robots and other forms of mechanization is the perceived threat from the increasingly pervasive use of AI, which was at the center of the Writers Guild of America and SAG-AFTRA months-long strike in 2023. Research by Ernst & Young in 2023 showed that 65 percent of the US workers surveyed said they were concerned about losing their jobs to AI. In addition to the perceived threat to employment, studies show that automation is also seen by workers as a threat to earnings.

7.3.2 *Automation and Senior-level Management*

Operations management, senior-level management, and company boards have generally viewed automation in terms of its ability to improve, and in some cases dramatically improve manufacturing efficiency and productivity, the quality of manufacturing functions (such as the consistency and precision of spot welding functions), the speed and flexibility

---

[54] Daron Acemoglu, "How many jobs do robots really replace?"

of manufacturing functions, the quality of components and products produced, and worker safety—and the ability of automation to achieve manufacturing functions that are difficult, dangerous, or in some cases impossible to achieve manually. For example, the first use of industrial robotics in the US auto industry occurred in 1961, when a GM factory in New Jersey installed a robot to lift hot pieces of metal from a die-casting machine; which was a worker-safety measure, and was not related to reducing the need for labor.

These operational benefits of automation notwithstanding, operations management, senior-level management, and company boards frequently use automation as a mechanism for reducing the need for labor—especially when they believe that their entity has been, or could be, held to ransom for what they see as unreasonable wage and benefits demands. For example, in 2023, during contract negotiations between UPS and the Teamsters union (which represented 340,000 UPS drivers and warehouse workers), 97 percent of the Teamsters members voted to authorize a strike. To avoid the strike, UPS agreed to wage and benefits increases for full-time and part-time workers, which resulted in some UPS drivers receiving as much as $170,000 in annual pay. Over the next 18 months, UPS made major investments in the automation of its warehouses and eliminated thousands of warehouse jobs.

7.3.3 Application

In almost all manufacturing strategies, the elements from this DP are used in a hybrid, because even the least automated manufacturing process includes some degree of mechanization, and even the most automated manufacturing processes include some manual component (such as visual inspections and the maintenance of tools, production lines, and production line robots). The decision facing executives and strategy teams is, therefore, the relative weight they decide to give to each element in the hybrid.

When using a manual & automated DP hybrid, some executives and strategy teams, and company boards and senior-level management, have attempted to avoid dependency on the manual element by overweighting the automated element. For example, in 1992, the chairman and CEO of GM, Roger Stemple, told Fortune magazine: "We put a tremendous amount of automation and electronics into our Cadillac plant in Hamtramck. And we couldn't run it because our people didn't understand what we were asking them to do. We literally had to stop the assembly line to get the reading and math skills up."[55]

In 2017, the CEO of Tesla, Elon Musk, announced that the automation of the Model 3 production line would make their Fremont plant the "factory of the future." But the production of the Model 3 was repeatedly delayed, and was then repeatedly suspended due to assembly line issues. In 2018, Musk said that automation had held back Model 3 production and that humans, rather than machines, were the answer—and that one reason Tesla had struggled to reach promised production volumes was because of the company's "excessive automation";[56] and, in a Twitter posting, Musk said that "excessive automation at Tesla was a mistake."[57]

7.4   Domestic and International

The effects of globalization, and the evolution of international supply chain management, have meant that almost all manufacturing operations include some nondomestic element; and even manufacturing operations that appear to be wholly domestic in most cases include some material or component that is sourced internationally. But, as used here, the international element from this DP refers to a company or business unit engaging in manufacturing operations that are outside its home country, through the use of foreign direct investment, or by accessing the benefits of FDI manufacturing through the use of arm-length or less-than-arm's-length international relationships[58] and the use of FDI-related international trade.

Because the domestic & international DP applies to the formulation of a wide range of manufacturing and marketing strategies, it could be

---

[55] Fortune, March 9, 1992.

[56] The Guardian, April 16, 2018. "Elon Musk drafts in humans after robots slow down Tesla Model 3 production."

[57] Posting on Twitter by Elon Musk, on April 13, 2018.

[58] These FDI alternatives are discussed in Sections 7.4.3.1 and 7.4.3.2.

argued that this dichotomous pair is a general core DP. It has been included as a manufacturing core DP, however, because the difficulties and downsides associated with the use of FDI in international manufacturing can be significantly more severe, and in many cases significantly more difficult to manage, than the issues that affect the conduct of international trade in marketing strategies. The use of the domestic & international DP as a marketing DP is discussed in Section 7.4.5.

7.4.1 Domestic

The domestic element from this DP has traditionally been, in most cases, the default element in the formulation of manufacturing strategies: executives and strategy teams, and senior-level management and company boards, often cite the need for control and other logistical reasons for preferring to have manufacturing functions conducted domestically—unless there is a compelling reason not to. The selection of the domestic element also avoids the difficulties and downsides that are associated with FDI manufacturing and FDI-related international trade.

7.4.2 International

There are, however, several factors that cause manufacturing executives and strategy teams in some cases to prefer the international element, or to combine domestic manufacturing and foreign manufacturing in a domestic-international hybrid.

These international upside factors include the cost and other operational advantages of manufacturing a product or component in a foreign country, which can include the lower cost of labor, the availability of specialized manufacturing skills, the proximity to materials that are used in the manufacturing process, avoiding or reducing the cost of shipping by manufacturing close to the market, and/or to avoid cost of importation tariffs. For example, Apple says the reason it uses the international element from this DP, and manufactures most of its products at non-US locations, is lower costs and the availability of specialized manufacturing skills; in 1931, GM began manufacturing cars in Australia, which was initially limited to the assembly of imported parts, but later included all manufacturing functions,[59] and, in 2024, 40 percent of the vehicles sold by GM in the US were assembled in other countries; and BYD Auto assembles some of its BYD 8TT all-electric semitrailer tractors in the US, in Lancaster, CA.

For entities that are engaged in the extractive industries (which include oil and gas exploration and production, coal exploration and mining, and mineral exploration, mining, and processing)—the dominant factor that drives the selection of the international element is the locations of oil, gas, coal, or mineral deposits.

7.4.3   *Application and Alternatives*

Because the domestic element from this DP is in many cases the default element, and because the manufacture of a product or component in one or more foreign countries can in some cases provide significant advantages, executives or strategy teams frequently include both elements in a domestic-international hybrid, and use FDI or access to FDI, together with international trade, to share a product's manufacturing functions between their entity's home country and one or more other countries. More than one-third of world trade occurs between companies and their FDI subsidiaries, or between a company's FDI subsidiaries; and 80 percent of world trade is by entities that are engaged in FDI.

In some cases, international intracompany manufacturing is facilitated by regional integration agreements, such as the *United States, Mexico, Canada Agreement* (USMCA), and by bilateral mechanisms such as the *Maquiladora Program*, which allows companies to conduct some of a product's manufacturing operations in the US and some in Mexico, and allows for the duty-free cross-border movement of products during manufacture.

When using both elements from this DP in a hybrid, executives and strategy teams must determine the weight they should give to each of the elements in the hybrid, and must decide on the form of the hybrid's international element: the FDI option or an FDI alternative.

---

[59] For the discontinuation of GM's manufacturing operations in Australia, see Chapter 2, Section 2.2.1.

7.4.3.1   The FDI Option

There are several downsides that come with using FDI as the international element from this DP. These downsides can be grouped into two main categories: (1) entry barriers to FDI and (2) post-entry barriers to FDI.

Entry barriers to FDI manufacturing include host-country industry and nationality access barriers, closed industries, restricted open industries, and equity ownership restrictions. Post-entry barriers that affect FDI manufacturing operations include host-country legislated barriers that apply to all foreign-funded companies, or are industry specific or company specific; host-country local-content requirements, human resources indigenization requirements, and other HR requirements that apply to FDI; host-country landownership restrictions, leasing restrictions, and contract-specific barriers to FDI; host-country performance requirements and FDI export quota requirements; host-country administrative barriers that affect FDI applications and approvals; host-country restrictions on the repatriation of earnings and capital; currency differences and other financial barriers that can complicate the conduct of FDI; the politicization of trade and/or foreign direct investment by a host-country government, and other forms of political risk.

7.4.3.2   FDI Alternatives

When selecting the international element from this DP, executives and strategy teams can limit the difficulties and downsides associated with the FDI option by using arm-length and/or less-than-arm's-length relationships[60] with host-country nationals. These FDI alternatives include (1) selecting the outsource element from the outsource & insource DP,[61] and using a company that is a host-country national as a contract manufacturer, and engaging in international outsourcing and international supply chain management; or (2) using the allied element from the alone &

---

[60] Less-than-arm's-length relationships are discussed in Chapter 10, Section 10.4.1.1.

[61] The outsource & insource DP is discussed in Section 7.2.

allied DP,[62] and entering into an international SA[63] with a manufacturer that is a host-country national. For example, Apple manufactures most of its products at non-US locations through a combination of arm-length and less-than-arm's-length alternatives. In some cases, arm-length and/or less-than-arm's-length relationships with host-country nationals can remove or greatly reduce the difficulties associated with the navigation of the entry barriers and post-entry barriers to FDI, and can reduce exposures to political risk.

7.4.4   *Political Risk*

In the conduct of international trade and/or FDI, the term *political risk* refers to an exposure of an entity to the possibility of politicized adverse treatment by the legislative, executive, and/or judicial branch of a host-country or home-country government. The term is also used when referring to politicized governmental actions that affect an entity engaged in the conduct of international trade or FDI. Political risk exposures and/or actions can apply to an entity, its shareholders, its assets, and/or its operations; and can be home-country specific, company specific, or industry specific. The severity of FDI-related political risk can range from the imposition of discriminatory fees, controls, or requirements by a host-country government to the expropriation or nationalization of a company's foreign direct investment.

In the past: (1) almost all political risk was exposure to an action by a host-country government; and (2) the severity of a company's exposure to political risk, and the possible adverse effects of that exposure, were relatively high for FDI, but were low for international trade. In the current era, however, a resurgence in the use of protectionist trade policies and practices has resulted in (1) an increase in home-country political risk (that is, an increased exposure to the adverse effects of actions by a company's home-country government), and (2) an increase in the severity of trade-related political risk.[64]

---

[62] The alone & allied DP is discussed in Chapter 6, Section 6.4.
[63] Strategic alliances are discussed in Chapter 6, Section 6.4.2; and in Chapter 10, Section 10.4.1.
[64] Davies and Chen 2023, 56–57, 87.

7.4.5   When Used as a Marketing DP

For the reasons discussed in Section 7.4, the domestic & international DP is included as a manufacturing core DP; but it can also be used by executives and strategy teams when they are formulating marketing strategies.

The reasons for selecting or not selecting the domestic element from this DP are similar for both manufacturing and marketing strategies. In both usages, the domestic element is in most cases the default option, and the advantages and disadvantages discussed in Section 7.4.1 can also apply to marketing.

These similarities, however, do not apply to the international element. When the international element is used in the formulation of manufacturing strategies, the focus is usually on FDI and/or FDI alternatives. When it is used in the formulation of marketing strategies, the focus is usually on international trade—and the governmental, intergovernmental, and non-governmental factors that regulate and facilitate the conduct of international trade. These factors include tariff barriers, non-tariff barriers, and other barriers to trade; provisions contained in the General Agreement on Tariffs and Trade, in other global instruments, and in regional and bilateral preferential trade agreements; the functionalities of the World Trade Organization, other global mechanisms, and regional trade blocks (which include free trade areas and customs unions); international standards, the harmonization of laws, and the settlement of international commercial disputes[65]; and the political risk exposures discussed at the end of the previous section.

---

[65] Davies and Chen 2023, 10.

CHAPTER 8

Marketing Core DPs

Contents

There is a large number of discipline-specific DPs that are used in the formulation of marketing strategies, by entities that market diverse products and services, in diverse industries, in diverse geographical areas. There are, however, three marketing core DPs that can be used in the formulation of all (or almost all) marketing strategies, which are discussed in this chapter: (1) production & market orientation, (2) primary & secondary demand, and (3) differentiation & segmentation.

During the formulation of marketing strategies, executives or strategy teams can select elements from the general core DPs discussed in Chapter 6, and from the marketing core DPs discussed in this chapter. They can then identify or create strategy-specific marketing DPs that reflect the policy goals and/or operational goals that are driving the formulation of the subject strategy, and select elements from those DPs.

8.1   Production Orientation & Market Orientation

Since the advent of marketing orientation in the 1960s and 1970s, marketing executives and strategy teams have been debating the relative merits of the elements from this DP, and (as discussed in Section 8.1.3) have been including and weighting both elements in a wide range of production orientation & market orientation hybrids.

8.1.1   Production Orientation

Production orientation sees and talks about a product in terms of how it is made, where it is made, and/or what it is made from. Production orientation is indicated by any reference to the materials or components used to make a product; the methods, processes, or tools/machinery used to make a product; the technology used in the design or manufacture of a product; and/or reference to the persons who make the product and/or to the product's place of manufacture. We are using production-oriented descriptors when we say a desk has a steel frame, that the frame is welded, that it is made by skilled craftspersons, and/or that it is made in Germany.

The production-oriented element can be used when marketing food, clothing, consumer products, household appliances, commercial or industrial products, or any other type of product. When a computer company says a product has Intel inside or a Liquid Retina display, when Gillette says its Mach 3 razor blades are platinum coated, when Procter & Gamble says its Crest toothpaste contains fluoride, when Midea says it makes the Toshiba-Macro compressors and all other components used in the manufacture of its air conditioners, and when Airbus says its A320 aircraft is assembled in Toulouse, France—these companies are saying what their products are made from, how they are made, and/or where they are made, and are using the production orientation element.

8.1.2   Market Orientation

Market orientation sees and talks about a product in terms of the benefits it provides to the customer and/or end user, and/or how it provides these benefits. We are using market-oriented descriptors when we say a desk is comfortable to sit at and use, is solid and stable, looks good, and will last a long time.

The market orientation element can be used when marketing food, clothing, consumer products, household appliances, commercial or industrial products, or any other type of product. When Gillette says its Mach 3 blades give a closer shave and last longer, when Procter & Gamble says its Crest toothpaste prevents cavities, and when Boeing says its 777 provides airlines with greater operating efficiencies—these companies are saying what their products do for the customer and/or end user, are using the marketing orientation element.

Although market orientation can be seen in how a product is presented, an important aspect of market orientation is that it drives product design and development. Before the advent of market orientation, most companies designed, developed, and manufactured products—then decided how to sell them. At that time, manufacturing preceded marketing: A company first made a product, then transferred the responsibility for selling the product to its distribution, advertising, and sales departments.

The advent of marketing orientation in the 1960s and 1970s transformed business thinking by saying that the process must begin with market research, not manufacturing. The proponents of market orientation argued that the product design and development process must begin by thinking about the needs, wants, and preferences of customers and end users; and that every step of the design and development of a product must be driven by (1) who will buy the product, (2) why they will buy it, and (3) how they will use it. This was transformational, because it put marketing (or at least some marketing functions) before manufacturing.

This aspect of market orientation can be seen by looking at the origins and evolution of many successful brands and companies. Market orientation argues that the fundamental reason for the success of a famous brand is not due simply to how the brand has been marketed, but is because the design, development, and manufacture of the products have been, and continue to be, driven by the needs, wants, and preferences of customers and end users.

8.1.3 Origins and Application

The term *market orientation* and its fundamental principles were developed in the United States. Until the 1960s, most companies in the US were heavily production oriented; they followed the European tradition, where making a better product meant making it from better materials and/or making it with better workmanship. In the 1960s and early 1970s, business-school faculty in the US developed market-oriented concepts and principles, which were embraced and implemented by many companies in many industries. During this period, market-oriented concepts and principles dominated marketing strategy, and marketing strategy dominated business thinking.

During the 1970s, marketing executives and strategy teams at Japanese companies followed the US marketing model and became more consumer centered, and embraced market-oriented concepts and principles (such as when Toyota and other Japanese companies included market orientation in their manufacturing strategies by including it as one of the three principal elements of Total Quality Management), and Japanese companies have, since the 1980s, been leading advocates and users of market orientation.

When the concepts and principles of market orientation were first introduced in the United States, production orientation was repudiated; and many proponents of market orientation insisted that advertising and promotional materials should not include any reference to production-oriented factors, on the grounds that production-oriented factors do not benefit the customer or end user. This purist approach to market orientation was, however, flawed, because many production-related factors benefit significantly the consumer and/or end user, and production-related factors can influence purchase decisions.

When a company says its razor blades are platinum coated, its toothpaste contains fluoride, or its computers have Intel inside or Liquid Retina displays, they are using the production orientation element from this DP. But in many cases, these production orientation factors are *market relevant*, because they provide support for a market-oriented claim. When Gillette says its blades are platinum coated, this provides the grounds for saying their blades will stay sharp longer, and will, therefore, continue to provide the end user with more and better shaves.

Because production-oriented factors can provide support for market-oriented claims, marketing strategies frequently include both elements from this DP in a hybrid, where the production orientation element is used to support the market orientation element.

8.2   Primary Demand & Secondary Demand

The primary demand element from this DP is used to increase an entity's sales of a product by increasing the size of the market for the product category; the secondary demand element is used to increase an entity's sales of a product by increasing the entity's market share of the product category.

8.2.1   Primary Demand

When the market for a product category is viewed as a pie chart, a company or business unit is using the primary demand element from this DP when it applies its marketing resources to increase the size of the pie. The primary demand element is used when a product has no direct competitors, which in this context refers to competitors in the same product category or the same market segment. If a company uses the primary demand element when it has less than 100 percent of a market, it will be using its marketing resources to create sales for its competitors, and will not be using those resources to protect and/or increase its market share.

Primary demand strategies, like all marketing strategies, are designed to persuade; but the advertising and promotion used in primary demand marketing is characterized by being informative, factual, and rational. In most primary demand strategies, the form and content of the message looks less like advertising and more like education. When Jeffrey Bezos created Amazon, he chose the primary demand element, and focused all of his marketing resources on educating book buyers about the benefits of buying online.

8.2.2   Secondary Demand

When the market for a product is viewed as a pie chart, a company is using the secondary demand element from this DP when it uses its marketing resources to increase the size of its piece of the pie. Most marketing strategies use the secondary demand element from this DP, because executives and strategy teams have learned that, when they control less than 100 percent of a market or market segment, the most effective use of marketing resources is to focus on maintaining and/or increasing their market share. Coca-Cola and Pepsi, Nestlé and Maxwell House, and Airbus and Boeing are all using the secondary demand element when they try to maintain or increase sales and/or market share of their brand of cola drinks, instant coffee, and passenger airplanes. All companies that manufacture and market cars use secondary demand strategies. In each of these examples, each of the companies applies its marketing resources to try to persuade prospective customers to buy its products, rather than buying products made by its competitors.

8.2.3   Characteristics and Application

As with all of the dichotomous pairs discussed in this book, both elements in this DP are situation specific. If a company has no direct competitors, it will select the primary demand element. When one or more competitors enter the market, the company must shift to the secondary demand element (or possibly to a primary demand & secondary demand hybrid).

In 1937, Nestlé's R&D laboratories in Switzerland invented instant coffee, which they called Nescafé, and the company invested heavily in attempting to persuade coffee drinkers in Europe, North America, and other parts of the world to drink instant coffee. When General Foods introduced its own brand of instant coffee (Maxwell House) in the US and then in Europe, Nestlé switched to the secondary demand element; it stopped promoting the benefits of instant coffee, and instead promoted the benefits of drinking Nescafé.

In some cases, secondary demand strategies have increased the size of the pie. For example, the secondary demand strategies used by cellular phone makers and service providers have increased the total demand for cell phones; and the secondary demand strategies used by the manufacturers of EVs have, in some countries, increased the total demand for electric vehicles.

8.2.4   Primary–Secondary Demand Ambiguity

The primary demand element is used when a product has no direct competitors. It can be argued, however, that all products have competitors; there is always an alternative product that addresses a particular consumer need or want. Even if there are no direct competitors from within the product category or market segment, there are indirect competitors from other product categories and other market segments.

When Bezos created Amazon, the company had no direct competitors in the online segment of the book market. But if we had drawn a pie chart of total book sales, it would have had slices indicating the market shares for online book sales, and for book sales by various types of bricks-and-mortar bookstores. So although Amazon can be cited as a quintessential example of a primary demand marketing strategy, it could be argued that, from the beginning, Bezos was using a secondary demand strategy to steal book sales and market share from the traditional bricks-and-mortar segment of the *total book sales* market.

8.3   Differentiation & Segmentation

The differentiation element from this DP engages the competition and argues that its product is *better*; the segmentation element avoids the competition by arguing that its product is *different*. As discussed in Section 8.3.3, in some marketing strategies there can be an overlap or interrelationship between the elements from this DP.

8.3.1   Differentiation

The purpose of a differentiation strategy is to maintain or increase sales of a product, and/or preserve and/or increase product market share, by engaging the competition. When a company uses a differentiation strategy, it attempts to achieve competitive advantage by showing that its product is *better* than a product offered by one or more of its competitors. The differentiating variable for a particular product can include: better design, better quality, better performance, better reliability and durability, and/or better price. When Boeing is marketing its 777, it is using a differentiation strategy when it says this airplane is able to fly further, and, therefore, provides airlines with greater operating efficiencies than the airplanes that are designed and built by Airbus.

In marketing strategy, a differentiator is a product attribute that says why and/or how the product is better than one or more competitors' products. A company may use differentiators that say its product is better designed, is made from better materials, is made with superior skills or machinery, is more reliable, is more available, is more prestigious to own, is easier and/or more fun to use, is supported by better after-sales service, or costs less to purchase, operate, and maintain. For a particular marketing strategy for a particular product, a company may use a combination of these and other differentiators.

8.3.2   Segmentation

When a company uses a segmentation strategy, it attempts to achieve competitive advantage by saying its product is *different* from the products made by its competitors. The primary advantage of segmentation is that it avoids engaging the competition. When Chrysler (which is now part of Stellantis) introduced its first minivans in 1983, and when Bezos created Amazon in 1994, they were each pursuing a product segmentation strategy. To avoid competing with other products in the motor vehicle market, Chrysler created a different category of motor vehicle that offered a different way of delivering transportation. By creating a new market segment, Chrysler had no direct competition for its Dodge Caravan and Plymouth Voyager minivan products; which allowed it to control 100 percent of the minivan market. This same advantage was repeated when Bezos created Amazon.

A company may prefer to use the segmentation element if it is participating in a highly competitive market, if the company's product holds a small market share, if the product has few or no differentiators (that is, if it has few or no competitive benefits), and/or if it is not possible to price the product competitively and still realize a profit. In some cases, an executive or strategy team will select the segmentation element from this DP because they want to avoid the cost, risk, and possible trauma of engaging in competitive marketing strategies. For many executives, however, segmentation is the ultimate silver-bullet marketing strategy—because it offers the bliss of no competition.

There are, however, two downsides to using the segmentation element from this DP. The segmentation element defines a product into an industry segment or subsegment that did not previously exist, which means there is no market for the new product—there are no existing customers. To address this downside, a company using a segmentation strategy must create a new market by implementing a primary demand strategy. This can have high financial and managerial costs, it can have high risks, and creating a new market takes time.

The second downside of segmentation strategies is that the relief from the discomfort of having to engage with competitors is in most cases temporary. If a company is successful at creating a new market for its new segmented product, competitors will enter this new market, and the company may be forced to change to a differentiation strategy. When this occurs, some companies have tried to argue that their product is better because it created a new product category and a new market. But customers usually do not care who invented a product category, and they do not make purchase decisions based on who invented the category.

Some segmentation strategies are more sustainable than others. The Reserve Fund, which invented the money market mutual fund in the US in 1971, now has more than 300 competitors for this financial product, and the Fund controls less than 1 percent of the market. Chrysler's minivan products now have many competitors, but Chrysler still holds almost 40 percent of the US minivan market (compared to its 7 percent share of the car market, and 11 percent of the sport-utility market). Amazon's on-line book-selling operations now has many competitors, but the company still holds a major share of the market.

8.3.3   Application

Using a differentiation element from this DP can be difficult, if the product has few or no discernable differentiators, if it is undifferentiable.

Undifferentiable products, such as wheat, rice, milk, iron, copper, and cotton are called commodities. In the history of marketing, executives and strategy teams have tried to differentiate commodities by attempting to exploit actual or invented differentiators, such as the on-product branding of Chiquita bananas.

An advantage of choosing the differentiation element, however, is that it allows a company to participate in an industry segment or subsegment that exists. It provides access to an existing market or market segment, and provides access to existing customers and end users.

In some cases, there can be an overlap or interrelationship between the two elements from this DP—when a company argues that its product is *better* (differentiation) because it is *different* (segmentation). When Chrysler introduced the minivan in the US, it was using a segmentation strategy: It was saying the minivan was different. But Chrysler was also using a differentiation strategy: It was saying that, for some people, the minivan's different design makes it a better form of transportation. And when Bezos invested huge resources to educate people about the benefits of buying books online, he was saying that online book-buying is not only *different* (segmentation) but, for several reasons, is also *better* (differentiation).

PART 4

Ancillary Factors

CHAPTER 9

Life-Cycle Positions

Contents

Executives and consultants who are engaged in the formulation of business strategies must have knowledge and skills relating to element selection, weighting, and configuration; and, if they are using the DPs method, must be familiar with the DPs discussed in Chapters 6, 7, and 8; and have the knowledge and skills needed to identify or create strategy-specific DPs, to select and weight DP elements, and to configure selected elements into mutually supportive and/or synergistic combinations. They must, however, also be familiar with two important ancillary factors that can affect the formulation, implementation, and sustainability of business strategies:

1. Product, industry, and company life-cycle positions; and
2. The zero-sum and plus-sum elements from the game theory dichotomy.

Life-cycle positions are discussed in this chapter; the elements from the game theory dichotomy are discussed in Chapter 10.

9.1   The Life-Cycle Concept

The term *life cycle* refers to the series of stages that organic entities pass through during their lives. When applied literally, the life-cycle concept is characterized by a sequence of stages that occur in a fixed hierarchical progression that is not reversible. The life-cycle concept allows for the possibility that the lives of some entities will end before they pass through all life-cycle stages. The life-cycle concept can also be applied to nonorganic entities that appear to follow a sequential pattern of development. When referring to nonorganic entity life cycles, the stages are usually referred to as phases. For example, when discussing the economic development of different nation-states, we can say China is in the growth phase of its economic-development life cycle, whereas the United States is in the mature phase.

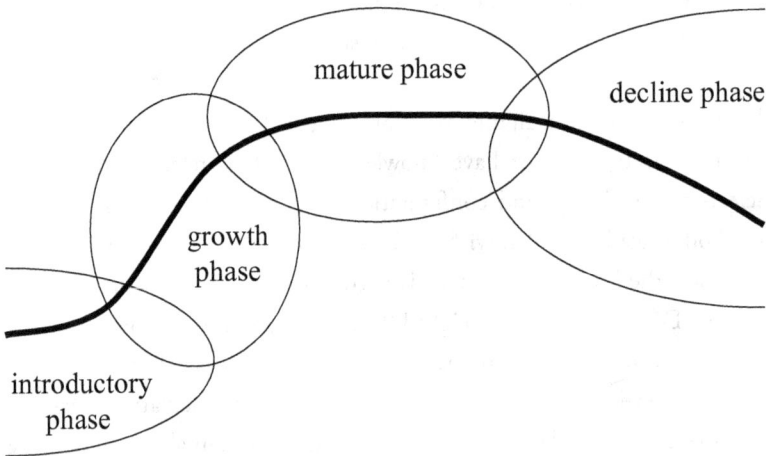

Figure 9.1. Life-cycle phases

In a *Harvard Business Review* article, 60 years ago, Ted Levitt extended the nonorganic application of the life-cycle concept to products, which he said can be seen as "passing through four recognizable stages," which he defined as: market development, market growth, market maturity, and market decline (Levitt 1965, 81). Since then, the product life-cycle principles discussed by Levitt have been extended to industries (industry life cycles) and to companies and business units (company life cycles); and his four recognizable stages are now usually referred to as the introductory phase, growth phase, mature phase, and decline phase.

9.2   Life-Cycle Positions

The term *life-cycle position* (LCP) refers to the position of a product (or service or project), industry, or company (or business-unit) in its life cycle. For example, when we say "the iPhone is in the mature phase of its life cycle," we are referring to its product LCP. Because each life-cycle phase covers a large area, it is common to refer to a product, industry, or company LCP as being in the early, middle, or late part of a phase—or being on the border between phases. When we say "Rivian Automotive is in the early growth phase of its life cycle," we are referring to its company LCP.

Business life cycles comply with most of the criteria from the life-cycle concept. In most cases, products, industries, and companies follow the same order of progression when passing through their life cycles. Also, consistent with the life-cycle concept, some product, industry, and company lives end before they have passed through all life-cycle phases.

There are two exceptions, where business life cycles do not comply with the progression criteria from the life-cycle concept. (1) In some cases, a product skips one or two life-cycle phases. For example, when a competitive or substitute product enters the market, a product in the growth phase of its life cycle may skip the mature phase and go directly to the decline phase. (2) In some cases, the progression of company life cycles does not comply with the nonreversible criterion discussed in Section 9.1. The possible reversibility of company and business-unit life cycles is discussed in Section 9.3.2.

One of the characteristics of business life cycles is that a product, industry, company, or business unit can be at different life-cycle positions in different geographical areas. For example, a product may be in the mature phase of its life cycle in economically developed countries, and in the growth phase in developing countries. A company or business unit may be in the early decline phase in its home country, in the late-introductory phase in a host country, and in the late-growth phase in another host country.

9.2.1   Identifying LCPs

Identifying the LCPs of new products, industries, companies, and business units is not difficult: They are at the beginning of the introductory phase. But after the product, industry, company, or business unit has moved beyond the beginning of the introductory phase, it is increasingly difficult to say with certainty where it is in its life cycle. This is due to several factors.

First, it is difficult or impossible to predict what will be the length and shape of a particular product, industry, or company life cycle; or to predict when a product, industry, company, or business unit will pass through each of its life-cycle phases.

Second, life-cycle phases are qualitative phenomena that do not lend themselves to quantitative measurement. In most cases, when we say a product, industry, company, or business unit is in a particular phase of its life cycle, we are making a tentative or provisional estimate (or guess) that is based on qualitative indicators. Third, as indicated by the ellipses in Figure 9.1, life cycles share large areas of overlap with the phases that precede and/or follow them. Fourth, the process of making, confirming, and/or refuting life-cycle estimates can be difficult because life-cycle phases are characterized by imprecise start and finish dates. For example, we can say "the iPhone is in the mature phase of its product life cycle," but because we cannot predict the duration of the smartphone industry life cycle, and because we cannot know if or when competitive products and/or substitute technologies will enter the smartphone market, we cannot determine the exact position of the iPhone in the mature phase of its product life cycle.

9.2.2   The Use of LCPs

Because it is difficult or impossible to predict the length and shape of current business-related life cycles, and because of the highly qualitative character of life cycles and LCP identification, many academicians (whose fields emphasize quantitative methods and empirical analysis) dismiss life-cycle phases and LCPs as totally unusable. But these limitations do not make LCPs less useful when formulating or analyzing business strategies. We frequently use imprecise assumptions, qualitative indicators, and/or other soft data when analyzing a huge range of personal, social, and professional situations. When we say China is in the growth phase of its economic-development life cycle, or that the US is in the mature phase, we are making these statements based largely on imprecise assumptions and qualitative observations, which are not less useful and usable because they are imprecise and qualitative.

Also, the imprecise and qualitative character of life cycles and LCPs is not of concern to most managers, executives, board members, and consultants who frequently make decisions and participate in the formulation of strategies using a combination of precise and imprecise assumptions, and quantitative and qualitative data.

9.2.3 *Life-Cycle Phase Dissonance*

Phase-dissonant combinations occur when a product, industry, or company LCP is in a different life-cycle phase than the other two; or when product, industry, and company life-cycle positions are all in different phases. Phase-dissonant combinations sometimes occur when young companies enter mature industries, or when mature companies enter industries that are in the early phases of their life cycles. For example, when Amazon created its AWS business unit in 2001, Amazon was in the mature phase of its company life cycle, the web-services segment of the IT industry was in the growth phase of its life cycle, and the services products that were being developed and marketed by the AWS business unit were in the introductory phases of their product life cycles.

In some cases, the reason companies enter into phase-dissonant combinations may be driven primarily by their need to make the quarterly numbers. In many cases, however, these combinations occur when a company is trying to avoid the dreaded decline phase of its company life cycle by migrating to growth industries, and/or by acquiring products, business units, or companies that are in the growth phases of their life cycles.

9.3 Company Life-Cycle Progression

All three business-related life cycles are important; they are not, however, equal in terms of their potential to threaten a company's continued survival, success, and sustainability. Every product has a finite life, but companies are able to develop and/or acquire new products. Also, the potentially debilitating effects of being in late-mature or declining industries is in some cases manageable, because companies can use divestiture, acquisition, spin-off, and start-up strategies to move into industries that are at earlier phases of their life cycles.

9.3.1 The Dreaded Decline Phase

In most cases, the life-cycles phase that is or should be of greatest concern to executives, senior-level management, and board members at mature companies is the decline phase of their products, industry (or industries) and company life cycles. This is because in many cases the greatest threat to companies and business units is not from their competitors and their competitors' products—but is from the decline phase of their products, industries, and company life cycles. Because companies can use various mechanisms to avoid or offset the downsides of product and industry decline phases, the most dreaded of the decline phases is the company decline phase.

There are many internal and external factors that can cause or contribute to a company's progression into the decline phase of its life cycle. These factors include the LCP of the company's industry area of domain (such as the photographic film industry decline and the demise of Kodak), the nature and degree of competition in the company's industry AOD (which in China has resulted in recent consolidations in the EV industry), the company's lack of suitable and sufficient resources (which, after 80 years of operations in the US, in 2025 led to the closing of all 800 Joann stores in 49 states), or a combination of these and other factors.

It is common to think that a company may be in the late-mature or decline phase of its company life cycle because of its age. But, except at the beginning of the introductory phase, the age of a company is not an indicator or cause of its company life-cycle position.

9.3.2 *Reversibility and Related Strategies*

When applied literally, the life-cycle concept is characterized by a sequence of phases that occur in a fixed hierarchical progression that is not reversible.[66] When the life-cycle concept is used in business, however, the nonreversible criterion does not apply to company life cycles—because in some cases the hierarchical progression of company life cycles can be reversed.

Companies can use build, buy, and alliance strategies[67] to move into growth industries; to acquire new core competencies, new technologies, new products and/or product lines, new markets and/or additional market share, motivated and experienced employees, company names, product brands, and company and product reputations; and to acquire business units or companies that are in the introductory, growth, or early mature phases of their life cycles. These DP elements or strategies can be used to retard or reverse company life-cycle progression.

---

[66] The LCP nonreversible characteristic is discussed in Section 9.1.

[67] Alliance strategies are discussed in Chapter 10, Section 10.4.1.

CHAPTER 10

The Game Theory Dichotomy

Contents

When executives and strategy teams are formulating corporate and business-unit strategies, they can select elements from the DPs categories discussed in Chapters 6, 7, and 8; but they also choose between zero-sum and plus-sum alternatives, which are two of the game theory categories that were developed by John von Neumann. The term *game theory* refers to situations where participants make decisions and take actions that affect each other. Game theory groups all interactive situations into three categories: zero-sum games, plus-sum games, and minus-sum games.

10.1   Game Theory Categories

The *zero-sum game* is a win-lose situation. Poker, chess, backgammon, and bridge are all examples of zero-sum games, "because the players' actions affect only the distribution, and not the size, of the pie" (McMillan 1992, 26). In each of these games, some players win and some lose, which results in the pie being redistributed among the players; but the size of the pie does not change, because the total of the wins equals the total of the losses: The total value of what leaves the game is the same as the total value of what was brought to the game, and the sum of the wins and the losses is zero.

The *plus-sum game* is a win-win situation. In a plus-sum game, the size of the pie is increased: The total value of what leaves the game is more than the total value of what was brought to the game, the sum of the wins and losses is positive.

The *minus-sum game* is a lose-lose situation. In a minus-sum game the sum of the wins and losses is negative, and the size of the pie is reduced.

10.2   Game Theory and the Formulation of Business Strategies

When executives and strategy teams are formulating business strategies, they choose between the first two game theory categories; they are engaged in the formulation of either a zero-sum strategy or a plus-sum strategy. This choice may not be intentional, and the executive or strategy team may or may not be familiar with game theory categories; but they have, in fact, chosen between the zero-sum and plus-sum elements of the game theory dichotomy.

10.3   Zero-Sum Strategies

In business, competitive strategies are structured as zero-sum games, where some players win and some lose, which results in the pie being redistributed among the players. For example, the cola wars between Coca-Cola and Pepsi in the United States have been a zero-sum game; the annual growth in the cola segment of the soft drink market in the US is negligible, which means that for either Coca-Cola or Pepsi to increase cola sales requires a corresponding loss in sales and market share by the other company. In zero-sum games, "for every winner there is a loser, and winners can only exist if losers exist" (Thurow 1980, 11).

10.3.1   The Zero-Sum Mindset

One reason that most business strategies are zero-sum games is because most business relationships in a market economy are competitive, rather than collaborative. A second reason may be due, at least in part, to the zero-sum mindset, which is the tendency for some executives and strategy teams to see all business situations as zero-sum phenomena (Davies 2000, 82).

The zero-sum mindset can be due to or affected by a combination of factors. These include an executive's social and cultural background; their motivational type and professional experience; and market-share data, the media, and the zero-sum character of competitive sporting events. The zero-sum mindset is also due to the fact that competitive strategy has come to dominate strategic thinking, and because competitive strategies are based on zero-sum assumptions. The emphasis on competitive strategy is so dominant that the terms *strategy* and *competitive strategy* are sometimes treated as if they were synonymous.

The zero-sum mindset can influence all areas of management and executive behavior. It can, however, be especially damaging in the strategy formulation process—because it restricts the choice of paths, options, and outcomes to those that are zero-sum. When executives and strategy teams are engaged in strategy formulation, the zero-sum mindset can be a form of selection bias,[68] which adversely influences the selection of elements from dichotomous pairs.

10.3.2   The Conversion of Zero-Sum Strategies

The zero-sum game is inherently unstable and is always in jeopardy of deteriorating into a minus-sum game, because a player's efforts to maximize their share of the pie can cause them to focus on preventing the other

---

[68] Selection bias is discussed in Chapter 3, Section 3.4.1.(c).

player from winning. This can produce similar responses by the other player, which can lead to a degeneration in the situation to the point where both players lose. When this occurs, the players have changed the game from zero-sum to minus-sum.

The conversion of a game from zero-sum to minus-sum is rarely addressed by game theory theoreticians, who assume that the zero-sum game is solely about distribution, not about the size of the pie. But this is only true if the game remains zero-sum. In the real world of business, human behavioral factors, operational pressures, and the effects of the zero-sum mindset can change the parameters of the game from zero-sum to minus-sum—because "seeking a larger share of the pie might result in reducing the total size of the pie" (McMillan 1992, 213).

10.4   Plus-Sum Strategies

Plus-sum strategies are strategies that are structured as a plus-sum game, where both or (in situations that include more than two participants) all players win. Even though the business environment in a market economy is generally seen as being entirely competitive, in practice it includes many collaborative plus-sum relationships, which provide executives and strategy teams with the opportunity to employ plus-sum alternatives. Most plus-sum strategies rely on the companies' complementary areas of domain and/or complementary core competencies.[69] Plus-sum principles can be applied in most intercompany relationships, if the focus of the relationship can be on asset generation and not on asset distribution, and if the relationship can be collaborative and not competitive.

10.4.1   Strategic Alliances

Plus-sum strategies can be used to create two-party (or in some cases, multiparty) structures that are referred to as *strategic alliances* (SAs), which are less-than-arm's-length relationships that are characterized by the merging

---

[69] Core competencies are discussed in Chapter 2, Section 2.4.4.

of complementary interests, the sharing of privileged information, and collaboration and cooperation. They are called strategic alliances, rather than alliances, to indicate that their purpose is to achieve one or more of an entity's policy or operational goals.

10.4.1.1 Less-Than-Arms-Length Relationships

The term *arm's-length* is borrowed from transfer pricing. For example, in the US, the Internal Revenue Service maintains an *arm's length standard* (under IRC [14] I.R.C. 482), which refers to transactions between unrelated parties and/or uncontrolled entities. The terms *arm's length* and *less-than-arm's-length*, as used in this book, refer to the relationship distance between entities that are engaged in business operations.

Arm's-length operational relationships include traditional sourcing agreements and traditional marketing, distribution, franchising, and licensing agreements between unrelated parties. The arm's-length agreement is characterized by its simple, unambiguous unrelated parties buyer-seller structure. Even if a manufacturer provides a supplier with a long-term supply contract and access to the factory floor to make just-in-time deliveries, provides a distributor with sales training, or allows a distributor extended terms for payment, this does not change the payment-for-goods-or-services arm's-length nature of the relationship.

Less-than-arm's-length relationships include nonequity agreements and joint ventures, including joint R&D agreements, joint product-development agreements, shared-knowledge sourcing agreements, joint marketing agreements, reciprocal-distribution agreements, standards-setting consortia, research consortia, and shared-knowledge and reciprocal franchising and licensing agreements. They also include equity agreements and joint ventures, including minority equity positions and debt-for-equity swaps that facilitate joint R&D, joint product development, and joint manufacturing and/or marketing; and equity and nonequity product-development agreements, technical assistance agreements, supply chain management agreements, manufacturing and/or marketing agreements, distribution agreements, and franchising and licensing agreements.

10.4.1.2   Other SA Characteristics

Strategic alliances between suppliers and manufacturers, manufacturers and distributors, and distributors and retailers can be structured as plus-sum games, because (1) the parties have different and complementary areas of domain and core competencies; (2) they want different things from the relationship; and (3) they share a mutual interest in increasing the size of the pie. When executives or strategy teams are formulating SAs and other collaborative business strategies, they have chosen the *plus-sum* alternative, and are engaged in the formulation of plus-sum strategies.

For example, manufacturer–distributor strategies can be structured as an SA because (1) increasing sales, market penetration, and market share benefits both parties; (2) in these relationships the manufacturer has core competencies in manufacturing and has products, which the distributor does not; and (3) the distributor has core competencies in distribution, and has a physical presence in a market segment, subsegment, or geographical area, which the manufacturer does not. In these SAs, the relationship between the manufacturer and the distributor can be structured to allow both parties to achieve what they could not achieve on their own. The plus-sum principles that apply to manufacturer/distributor SAs also apply to SAs that include manufacturers and suppliers.

10.4.1.3   SA Partner Risk

The multiple advantages of SAs notwithstanding, all SAs come with an inescapable downside, which is called *partner risk*—which is the exposure of an SA partner to opportunistic behavior by the other partner (Davies 2000, 10). SA partner risk often increases when SAs are in the late mature or decline phase of their life cycles, and can be exacerbated by SA partner angst, which can be due to an SA partner's perceived need for control, to the performance of an SA being less than was anticipated, to the presence of the zero-sum mindset, and/or to AOD convergence.

SA partner angst can increase partner risk if an SA partner believes that the other partner is deriving a disproportionate benefit from the alliance, if senior-level management believes that it will not receive the anticipated ROI or, worse, if they believe they may lose all or part of their operational and/or financial investment. In some cases, SA partner angst can cause a partner's senior-level management to limit their operational and/or financial commitment to an SA, and/or to attempt to recoup at least part of their actual or anticipated financial losses. When these actions include opportunistic behaviors, they can precipitate a further deterioration in the performance of the SA, can convert the SA from a plus-sum game to a zero-sum game, and can trigger and then perpetuate a minus-sum downward spiral.

10.4.1.4 Area of Domain Convergence

Strategic alliances that include manufacturers and distributors, or manufacturers and suppliers, are usually based on the assumption that both companies will maintain the difference in their areas of core competency and the differences in their areas of domain. But manufacturers, distributors, and suppliers frequently expand their areas of core competency, and in some cases change their AOD. When a company in a strategic relationship moves into the other company's AOD, this can be referred to as *area of domain convergence*.

Area of domain convergence often occurs in SAs when one of the partners engages in vertical integration.[70] A distributor may engage in backward vertical integration into manufacturing; a supplier may engage in forward vertical integration into manufacturing; or a manufacturer may engage in forward or backward vertical integration by expanding its AOD into a distributor's or supplier's area of domain. In any of these or similar situations, AOD expansion can cause the companies in an SA or other strategic plus-sum relationship to become competitors. When this occurs, the relationship between the companies changes from plus-sum to zero-sum, and can result in the conversion of an SA from a plus-sum game to a zero-sum game, which can increase the exposures of one or both SA partners to partner risk.

10.4.2 Sustaining Plus-Sum Strategies

The risk that a company's plus-sum strategies will be converted to zero-sum strategies cannot be eliminated; it can, however, be managed and

---

[70] Vertical integration is discussed in Chapter 6, Section 6.2.1.

mitigated by establishing and maintaining plus-sum structures and plus-sum environments.

10.4.2.1   Plus-Sum Structures

Like strategies, organizational structures can be classified as zero-sum, plus-sum, or minus-sum. When used in the implementation of plus-sum strategies, zero-sum structures can be disastrous. Because the zero-sum game is a game of pure conflict, a zero-sum structure sets up financial, personnel, logistical, and operational situations that are inherently adversarial and confrontational—which create a win-lose contest, which can result in the demise or destruction of even the best-designed plus-sum strategies.

The use of a plus-sum structure counters the zero-sum mindset by supporting the strategy with plus-sum logistical and operational factors that affect and motivate plus-sum thinking and behaviors. Because an organization's work environment is influenced by its organizational structure, a plus-sum structure facilitates the establishment of a plus-sum environment.

10.4.2.2   Plus-Sum Environments

In a zero-sum environment, possibilities are evaluated against zero-sum criteria, decisions are based on win-lose assumptions, and actions are motivated by the belief that the size of the pie is fixed. In a plus-sum environment, possibilities are evaluated against plus-sum criteria, decisions are based on and driven by win-win assumptions, and executives and senior-level management see each element in a strategy as an opportunity that will (to varying degrees and usually in different ways) benefit all participants.

When formulating corporate and business-unit strategies, a plus-sum environment counters the possible presence, threat, and/or effects of a zero-sum mindset by supporting a corporate or business-unit culture in which policy and operational goals, and strategy-related decisions, are driven by plus-sum beliefs, plus-sum assumptions, and plus-sum criteria.

Bibliography

Aristotle. "Metaphysics 1013a." Aristotle in 23 Volumes, Vols. 17, 18, trans. Hugh Tredennick. Harvard University Press; William Heinemann Ltd. 1989. https://www.perseus.tufts.edu/hopper/text?doc=Perseus%3Atext%3 A1999.01.0052%3Abook%3D5%3Asection%3D1013a.

Borden, Neil H. "The Concept of the Marketing Mix." In *Science in Marketing*, edited by George Schwartz. John Wiley, 1964.

Culliton, James W. *The Management of Marketing Costs*. Division of Research, Graduate School of Business Administration, Harvard University, 1948.

Davies, Warnock. *Partner Risk: Managing the Downside of Strategic Alliances*. Purdue University Press, 2000.

—. "Understanding Strategy." *Strategy & Leadership*. Volume 28, Number 5, September / October 2000.

Davies, Warnock, and Clive G. Chen. *International Trade and FDI: An Advanced Introduction to Regulation and Facilitation*. Business Expert Press, 2023.

Hamel, Garry, and C. K. Prahalad. "Strategic Intent." *Harvard Business Review*, May–June, 1989, 63–76.

Hofstede, Gert. *Culture's Consequences: Comparing Values, Behaviors, Institutions and Organizations Across Nations*. 2nd ed. Sage Publications. Country individualism index. 2001. https://hbr.org/1989/05/strategic-intent-2

Levitt, Theodore. "Exploit the product life cycle." *Harvard Business Review*, November–December, 1965, 81–94. https://hbr.org/1965/11/exploit-the -product-life-cycle

McMillan, John. *Games, Strategies and Managers*. Oxford University Press, 1992.

Merriam-Webster.com Dictionary, s.v. "governance." Accessed April 25, 2025. https://www.merriam-webster.com/dictionary/governance.

Schneider, Jordan, Angela Shen, Irene Zhang, et al. "DeepSeek: The Quiet Giant Leading China's AI Race." *China Talk*, November 27, 2024. https://www .chinatalk.media/p/deepseek-ceo-interview-with-chinas.

Thurow, Lester. *The Zero-Sum Society*. Basic Books, 1980.

von Neumann, John, and Oskar Morgenstern. *Theory of Games and Economic Behavior*. Princeton University Press, 1944.

About the Author

Warnock Davies is a consultant, with extensive experience in the formulation and implementation of corporate and business-unit strategies at major multinational corporations and midsize companies in a wide range of industries, in the United States and other countries, and in other areas of corporate governance. He has provided advice and assistance to senior-level management and boards of directors in the US and other countries; has held senior-level executive appointments in the private sector; and has served as a consultant with governments and nonprofit entities. He has held full-professor faculty appointments at universities in the US and other countries; has directed and taught in graduate programs, executive programs, and in-company seminars; holds a PhD and other graduate degrees from Tufts and Harvard Universities; and is the author of articles and books on business strategy, international business, and corporate governance.

The author can be contacted at StrategyCG@outlook.com. He would especially like to hear your comments concerning the book, or if you have found an error in the text.

Index

www.ingramcontent.com/pod-product-compliance
Lightning Source LLC
Chambersburg PA
CBHW061319220326
41599CB00026B/4957